FINESSIN' FINANCES

Sammy,

Thank you for the support !

FINESSIN'
FINANCES

THE REFRESHINGLY ENTERTAINING GUIDE
TO PERSONAL FINANCES

Stefon Walters

Finessin' Finances: The refreshingly entertaining guide to personal finances

© 2019 Stefon Walters

ISBN: 978-0-578-45349-1

Front cover image by Kenrick Jobe
Edited by Stanton Parker II
Book design by Stewart A. Williams | stewartawilliams.com

First printing edition 2019.

Published by Just Believe Company

For Mark Walters
the person who taught me to always believe.
Rest in peace, Pops.

CONTENTS

INTRODUCTION

Let's start by addressing the elephant in the room: finances are boring as hell. Some people would rather watch paint dry in a windowless room than to read about finances — and honestly, I don't blame them. Far too often, people go online looking for answers to their financial questions, only to end up more confused than they originally started. A simple question leads to overcomplicated explanations that read more like a foreign language.

This doesn't have to be (and shouldn't be) the case. There's no reason why finances — considering how important they are — should be misunderstood by so many people. The effects of this are very real, and they aren't created equal. Being a minority in America is already an uphill battle; there's definitely no denying that. Being a minority in America lacking financial literacy is like trying to get up a hardwood hill wearing socks.

Economic inequality in America is nothing new. It's been around for centuries and has been researched and discussed for decades. Yet, nothing has changed. In fact, it has only gotten worse. Far too often, these conversations focus on income inequality and skim over the overarching problem of wealth inequality. Wealth, in my opinion, is the most important measure of economic well-being, and the gap is far wider than the income gap. Wealth allows people to open businesses, get debt-free educations, survive during periods of unemployment, and withstand unexpected expenses.

There's a direct correlation between wealth and economic security. High income, unfortunately, doesn't always correlate to financial security. Making a lot of money doesn't mean much when you have a lot of expenses and debt.

Me telling you that there's a wealth gap in America would probably be as surprising as me telling you that water is wet, or that a Martin Luther King Boulevard was in the hood. However, you may be surprised to find out just how bad the gap is, and how much it's widening. Studies have shown that for every $100 in White family wealth, Black families hold just over $5. The median wealth of White families is $134,000. The median wealth of Black families is $11,000. Take a second to process that.

Even after beating the odds and climbing the economic ladder, minorities have a tougher time staying there. There's an old saying in Black communities: When White America catches a cold, Black America catches pneumonia. This applies to many aspects of life, but nowhere is this more evident than when looking at economic inequality. Regardless of what some old White man in a suit on Fox News may try to tell you, financial hardships aren't created equal. When shit hits the fan – whether in the market or personally – the results can be disproportionately disastrous for minorities at the bottom of the economic ladder. Of course, by no means am I saying that White Americans don't experience any financial hardships; life happens to everybody. I'm just saying that when you compare the two: one is a torn ACL injury and one is a sprained ankle. I'm sure you can guess which is which.

The issue of economic inequality is without a doubt systemic. You could start and finish watching *Titanic* faster than you could finish reading a list of all the things contributing to the problem. There's no single solution to reducing the wealth gap; a systemic problem has to be addressed with systemic changes. The wealth gap doesn't exist because some folks just so happened to make better financial decisions than others.

Financial literacy by itself won't solve the problem. Knowing how stocks work won't stop Black folks from getting paid $0.61 for every $1 that their White peers earn, and knowing what a 401(k) is won't stop predatory lending in predominantly Black neighborhoods. I'm not naive enough to think that.

I do, however, know that considering the systemic challenges we're up against, it's more important than ever to be financially literate. It's no coincidence that folks who are the most at-risk for being economically disadvantaged are also the groups lagging behind in financial literacy. Ignorance may be bliss, but financial ignorance is dangerous and expensive.

Time and time again, research shows us that folks with financial knowledge tend to be better savers, make better investment decisions, and manage their money better for retirement. So why don't more people (particular minorities) invest more into financial literacy? It's not because folks enjoy being economically disadvantaged and just don't give a damn about finances. It oftentimes comes down to simply not knowing.

Even for those who want to educate themselves about finances, there's a huge disconnect in how the information is presented. The majority of things written about finances are filled with jargon you'd put on your resume to gas up your past job experiences. A person stocking shelves at Walmart somehow becomes an "Inventory Control Specialist" and a paperboy somehow becomes a "Media Distribution Manager."

It's time to switch the finance game up.

This book is not a get-rich-quick, "turn $500 into $5,000 overnight" type of guide. I wouldn't still be sneaking Sprite in my water cups at restaurants if I knew those secrets.

This book is not an in-depth investment guide. I'm not a young Warren Buffett with melanin or anything like that. I won't be recommending specific stocks or giving false promises on returns. The last thing I need is for people to be dragging my name through the mud like I'm the new Bernie Madoff or Jordan Belfort.

Last but not least, this book is not the same dull finance content that you're used to. I'm not here to stroke my ego and see how many big words I can fit into a paragraph, and I won't bombard you with a bunch of numbers and calculations. Folks who actually like math can be added to the unofficial list of untrustworthy people — along with club promoters and used car salesmen.

This book is, however, a breath of fresh air. You will learn, you will laugh, and more importantly, you will have a lot of the foundations needed to start making better financial decisions.

Let the Finessin' begin!

"I'm not saying I'm gonna rule the world or I'm gonna change the world, but I guarantee you that I will spark the brain that will change the world. And that's our job, It's to spark somebody else watching us."
—TUPAC SHAKUR

CHAPTER ONE

CREDIT

*"You wanna know what's more important than
throwin' away money at a strip club? Credit."*
—JAY-Z

We all have that one friend that we're hesitant to lend things to, no matter what it is. We may love them like Mexicans love tequila, but we know that once we let them borrow something it's as good as gone. I've even had folks borrow something for so long that I had to borrow it back as if it wasn't mine. Life's funny like that.

Lenders, however, don't have the luxury of knowing their customers on a personal level. They rely on your credit report to determine your likelihood of paying back what you borrowed. Good credit — much like trust, and that Summer body you've been "working on" for some time now — takes a while to develop, but very little time to destroy. To be fair, a low credit score isn't the end of the world. You can still live a "normal" life with bad credit; it's just not easy or cheap. If you're Black or Latino, it's even harder and more expensive. Even after the Federal Fair Housing Act supposedly banned racial discrimination in lending decisions, Blacks and Latinos continue to be denied lines of credit at higher rates than White people with the same qualifications. Credit inequality is a real thing.

You might not be able to defeat the racist powers that be, but you can at least put yourself in a position to have the best score possible. Control what you can control.

CREDIT REPORTS

Credit reports come from one of three credit bureaus: Experian, TransUnion, or Equifax. These companies collect, update, and store credit histories for the majority of consumers.

It's important to understand that your credit report and your credit score are not the same. Your 3-digit credit score is calculated by what's on your credit report and the three credit bureaus score this number differently. Your actual credit report may vary slightly (although it's not common) by credit bureau as some lenders may only report to one or two credit bureaus; instead of all three.

You can receive a free copy of your credit report from each of the three credit bureaus once every 12 months. Don't confuse this with once per year, though. If you order a copy in August of one year, you won't be able to get another free copy until August of the next year; not January 1st.

Lenders and various other companies periodically send your financial-related information to the credit bureaus. This information is used to determine your credit-worthiness. There are four types of information you can find on your credit report:

1) Identity information. Your personal information — such as your name, Social Security number, address, and birthdate — are a part of your credit report. Thankfully, this information isn't used to calculate credit scores. Can you imagine taking a credit score hit because you had a black ass name like Tyrone or Leroy?

2) Credit accounts. Credit cards, student loans, auto loans, mortgages, and such accounts are a large portion of your credit report. Entries

contain information like the accounts credit limit, loan amount, current balance, the age of account, and more importantly, your payment history.

3) Inquiries. This section will contain information about the companies that have pulled a copy of your credit report for lending purposes. There are two different types of inquiries: soft and hard. Hard inquiries have a greater impact on your overall score. Examples of each are provided below:

    a. A hard inquiry would be used when applying for a mortgage or credit card. Lenders should notify you when a hard-inquiry is being completed. Multiple inquiries of the same kind, if completed within a short period of time, will not impact your score. This allows for shopping around for the best rates.

    b. A soft inquiry would be when someone wants to determine what you may qualify for, in terms of credit. A store credit card quote may fall in this category; prior to actually applying for the account.

4) Collections and bankruptcy information. Hopefully, you won't have many (or better yet, any) of these, but it happens. Past due accounts that have been turned over to a collections agency and any filed bankruptcies will be listed on your report. These items are harder to remove than red wine out of a white carpet and have a great impact on your score.

While there are different types of credit scores out there, the most important one is your **FICO** score – it's the most widely used. Roughly 90% of all lending decisions are made using your FICO score. It stands for Fair Isaac Corporation, which is derived from the founders' names Bill Fair and

Earl Isaac. Their company has become the financial industry's standard for credit. Since mama raised a nice southern gentleman and I don't want you embarrassing yourself in public, I'll go ahead and let you know it's pronounced like FIE-CO, not fee-co. You're welcome.

BENEFITS

Before we dive into what credit is, how it's calculated, how to build it, and so on, it's important to stress why having a good credit score even matters. Considering that the journey to having great credit isn't the smoothest, knowing why you should care about it can help maintain your focus.

Here are a few of the benefits of having a good credit score:

- Greater loan approval probability. You may find yourself in a situation where you need to take out a loan. It could be for personal reasons, or it could be for business reasons. Either way, you need money that somebody else has, and your credit score will be a huge factor in determining if they're willing to give it to you. Think about it, would you lend money to somebody who had a history of turning into Casper the Broke Ghost when it's time to pay it back? Albert Einstein once said, "The definition of insanity is doing the same thing over and over again, but expecting different results."

- Lower interest rates. Your interest rate is the cost you pay for borrowing money. The better your credit score, the lower your interest rates are. It's pretty straightforward. It may not seem like that big of a deal, until you realize how much more people end up paying in interest throughout the life of a loan. A few percentage points could result in a substantial amount of additional money coming out of your pocket. In severe cases, such as payday loans, the interest can exceed the original amount of the loan. That's highway robbery.

- Better credit cards. Credit cards can be crucial to your journey towards excellent credit; there's no denying that. Once an excellent credit score is achieved, you will gain access to exclusive credit cards that have very attractive perks. You'll get access to cards with higher spending limits, dope rewards, and even cash back on purchases. Credit cards will be covered in-depth in the next chapter.

- Avoid security deposits. Companies often require people with unestablished or bad credit to pay a security deposit, just in case they decide not to pay their bill. We all know how folks love to go missing when they owe you money. When they need cash, they'll pop up on you like a pimple on prom night, but when it's time to pay it back they're in witness protection all of a sudden. How convenient. The deposit is a means for the lending company to have some trust in the overall transaction. The same principle applies to collateral. Having established credit reassures companies that you're financially-responsible and helps them assess the likelihood of you paying your bill in-full and on-time. Since this makes you less of a risk for the company, many will often waive the security deposit in its entirety. These waivers could easily end up saving you a few hundred dollars.

- Higher credit limits. A good credit score will not only give you access to higher credit card limits (which can be a blessing or a curse, depending on how responsible you are), but it will also increase the loan amounts that a bank or other financial institutions will provide to you. Having a higher credit limit can be beneficial for two main reasons: it increases your access to funds in the event of an emergency, and it also increases the amount of money that it takes to push your credit utilization past the ideal 30%. There will be more on credit utilization in the coming chapters.

- More robust housing options. The increasing trend is that landlords are including credit checks as part of their application process. Having a bad credit score is a quick way to receive a "Sorry, but…nah" from a landlord — especially if your credit report has an eviction or past due rental payments on there. If you have one (or God forbid, both) of those on your credit report, you might as well save yourself the application fee and approach the landlord directly to explain your situation and plead your case.

• Better auto insurance rates. When you think of companies who rely on your credit report to make informed decisions, insurance companies aren't typically one of the first to come to mind. You'd be surprised at how many people don't realize just how much your credit report can affect your auto insurance rate. According to Nationwide, 92% of insurers consider your credit when deciding your premium. Unlike the traditional credit score used by financial institutions and lenders, insurance companies use credit-based insurance scores. As the insurance industry grows, their ability to predict liability based on demographic information is also increasing. For example, accountants are typically safer than stunt men. During a side-by-side comparison, you may notice a difference in the quotes – keeping all other variables the same. Insurance companies believe that people with bad credit are more likely to file more claims, which is why they end up with higher premiums.

CREDIT SCORE RANGE

If you don't know your credit score or don't have a recent copy of your credit report, now would be a good time to get it. You can head over to annual-creditreport.com to receive free copies of your credit report from the three major credit bureaus.

Now that we've covered some of the benefits of good credit, we should define what a good credit score is. After all, 'good' is fairly relative. Credit scores range from 300 to 850 and can be interpreted using the following scale:

300-579: Pretty damn bad. I'd rather walk through a Los Angeles Crip neighborhood wearing all red or fight a coked-up Mike Tyson in his prime than to loan somebody in this range some money. Don't get discouraged if you're in this range, better days are ahead!

580-649: Ehhh-ish. People in this range are as trustworthy as people who choose blue cheese over ranch for their wings. I wouldn't quite fight Mike Tyson before loaning them money, but I'd definitely consider running a 5K race barefoot first.

650-699: Good. You can view this range like bottom-shelf liquor or Franzia boxed wine. Your preference should be to avoid it, but it will definitely get the job done out of necessity. You should want better for yourself though.

700-749: Very good. Once you've reached this range, you can start to feel a little more confident. You aren't quite where you want to be, but you're well on your way.

750-850: Very damn good. If your score is in this range, salute! You're where you need to be. Now the goal is to stay there.

As of 2018, the average credit score in America was 704. The average credit score for someone looking to buy a house was 728, and all groups except Black people had an average score higher than 700.

CREDIT SCORE FACTORS

Now that you know your score, you may be wondering how that number is calculated. There are five main factors that determine your credit score. They are listed here in order of importance:

- Payment history (35%): Needless to say, your payment history is the most critical aspect of your credit report. A history of late or missed payments is obviously a red flag. If you run off on the plug once, you'll do it twice; the past is often a good predictor of the future. Lenders want to see that you can make your payments in-full and on-time.

Late payments only affect your credit score for about two years, but will physically remain on your report for seven years. Luckily for a lot of people, lenders understand that shit happens and they won't typically report a late payment to the credit bureaus unless it's more than 30 days late. If you remember on the 15th that your credit card payment was due on the 12th, then you won't have to worry about your credit score being affected. You'll just have to take those late payment fees on the chin and keep it moving.

- Credit utilization (30%): This is a fancy way of saying "out of all the credit you have available to you, how much are you using?" For example, if you have a credit card with a $1,000 spending limit, and you spend $200 of that, your credit utilization is 20%. You should always strive to keep this number below 30%.

Credit utilization is the one factor that many people overlook when it comes to their credit score. Paying your credit card bill in full each month is very important, but staying below 30% credit utilization throughout your billing cycle is vital as well.

Here are some tips:

If you can't reasonably keep your balance below 30% at all times, find out when your credit card company reports to the credit bureaus and try to pay your balance down before that date.

You'd think that all companies would report to the credit bureaus at the same time — you know, like the first or last day of the month — but that would be too easy and simple, wouldn't it?

Set balance alerts. It's 2019. Even your grandma who's still using a flip phone like drug dealers in *The Wire* can set-up balance alerts. You can get them via text or email. You don't even need a smartphone. If you're smarter than me, then you'll set it up to get alerts before you hit the 30% mark. Give yourself some breathing room.

If you're like the majority of people and it's hard for you to stop spending, ask for a credit limit increase on your card(s). This isn't the best option, but it works if you're disciplined. If your limit is $1,000 and you usually spend $500 every month, a credit limit increase to $2,000 would take your credit utilization from 50% to 25%. An increase doesn't mean you can go from eating Jimmy John's to eating Fogo de Chão. Just because your credit limit increased doesn't mean your paycheck did. Stay focused.

• Length of credit history (15%): Just like jobs prefer people with experience, lenders prefer folks who have a history of dealing with credit. Companies like FICO typically look at the age of your newest and oldest accounts, and the average age of all of your accounts. The thought is that the longer the credit history, the more accurate a lender can be in determining somebody's credit-worthiness.

If you're just now starting to build credit, it takes six months of at least one account reporting to the credit bureaus to be able to produce a credit score.

Because having older accounts on your credit report is beneficial, always think twice before closing out an old account; especially if it's a credit card. You don't have to use it, but having it on your credit report can work in your favor. Not only will it help in regards to your credit history length, but it can also serve the purpose of increasing your total amount of available credit. Consider just hiding it from yourself and put it somewhere you'll never look – like that one drawer in the kitchen that's filled with random items like fast food restaurant sauce packets and playing cards.

- Credit mix (10%): Having different types of accounts on your credit report is seen as a positive sign. It shows that you can multi-task financially. FICO's scoring model takes into consideration the number of accounts on someone's credit report, as well as the variety of account types. The different account types can be installment loans (like student loans and car loans), mortgage loans, credit cards, retail cards, gas station credit cards, and more.

I don't want you to read this and think that you need to head to the nearest Macy's and 7-Eleven and apply for their respective cards because you feel like you need to have a bunch of accounts on your credit report. That's just not smart, dawg. Aside from the fact that your credit score takes a slight hit with every hard inquiry, there's a real chance that you won't know how to manage them all responsibly. As a result, you will end up hurting your score instead of improving it. That's hustlin' backwards.

- Recent Inquiries (10%): When it comes to your credit report, there are two types of inquiries that you should familiarize yourself with: hard and soft inquiries.

Hard inquiries are the most important and occur when a lender, such as a bank or credit card company, checks your credit report to assist them in making a lending decision.

Whenever you encounter a hard inquiry on your credit report, your credit score temporarily drops a few points. Hard inquiries stay on your credit report for about two years, but they stop affecting your credit score after a few months, so don't worry too much. You still want to make sure to limit the number of hard inquiries within a short time period. When you apply for a lot of different credit lines within a short period, lenders see this as a red flag because it's assumed that if you need additional lines of credit then you're more at-risk of not paying off your existing debts. Three to five inquiries within a 2-year period is average. Less is better.

On the other hand, soft inquiries occur when your credit report is pulled for non-lending purposes. Often times these won't even show up on your credit report. Examples include mobile apps that allow you to check your credit score, credit card companies that "pre-qualify" you for particular offers, and employers that run background checks as part of their employment process.

BUILDING CREDIT

When it comes to building your credit, it can really be a Catch-22. On one end, you need good credit when applying for credit cards and loans. On the other end, you can't really establish credit without credit cards and loans. It's like trying to gain experience for a job even though jobs turn you down for not having any experience. Sound familiar?

Here are a few key ways you can begin your credit journey without needing a credit card:

Get a co-signer

I'ma keep it real with you. Outside of your parents, not many people with good sense are going to co-sign a loan for you. But, if you're one of the lucky ones who can find a co-signer, then you're in luck as they can be very beneficial. A co-signer takes on as much responsibility as you when it comes to making sure your loan is paid back in full. Your debt is their debt. This lowers the risks for the lender; specifically if the co-signer has established credit.

Nobody is gonna loan somebody with bad or no credit money just because somebody with bad or no credit co-signed them.

Apply for a credit-builder loan

Credit-builder loans are exactly what their name suggests: loans given with the intent of helping someone build their credit. The amount of these loans are relatively small and usually don't go much higher than $1,500. Even though it has the word "loan" in its name, credit-builder loans don't quite work like the traditional loans that most people are familiar with.

As you can imagine, credit-builder loans don't require good credit for approval (that would be ass-backwards). The lenders only care that you're bringing in enough income to pay it off.

There are three main types of credit-builder loans:

1) Pure credit-builder loan

With this type of loan, the lender puts however much the loan amount is into a locked savings account and you can't get access to it until the full amount is paid off. Even though you're paying on something you technically haven't received yet, these kinds of loans are clutch because you don't need to have money up-front to secure the loan. At the end of the loan's period, you'll have a nice chunk of change waiting on you and you will have made some progress in establishing credit.

2) Standard secured loan

With standard secured loans, the loan is "secured" by the amount someone has in a particular savings account because it will be used as collateral. The account in question will be frozen and the funds will be released in increments as you pay down the loan amount. The one thing to consider here is if you have the money to put down without needing it throughout the life of the loan. You are essentially borrowing money from yourself, and paying interest on it. Consider the interest rates before applying for this loan. Feel free to consult with a professional, if you are unsure that this loan is right for you.

3) Unsecured loan

Unsecured loans are closer to the typical traditional loans that you're probably used to hearing about or dealing with. These types of loans are like payday loans except much, much better. Payday loans are a bigger scam than Flat Tummy Tea.

You apply for the loan and receive the money right there on the spot. It's more instant than grits. You pay off these loans as you would any other loan.

It's worth noting that credit-building loans are usually given out by small banks and credit unions. You shouldn't expect to be able to walk into a multi-national financial institution and receive a credit-building loan — the chances are slimmer than a stick figure. Save yourself that humbling experience and look at more local institutions. Smaller banks and credit unions have more of a vested interest in seeing their local communities flourish, so these loans are more common amongst them.

As with almost all decisions involving your personal finances, you should take some things into consideration before jumping off the porch and grabbing one of these loans for the hell of it.

If you're currently having trouble paying your bills, then taking out one of these loans isn't your best bet, fam. Trust me on this one. The point is literally to build credit — you're hustlin' backwards if you take out one of these loans and end up missing payments or defaulting on it. Everything (good and bad) gets sent to credit bureaus, so don't get caught slacking.

During the period of your loan, you may get the urge to go ahead and pay it all off. Don't do that. I usually hate repeating myself, but again: don't do that. Credit takes time. Don't get impatient and block your own goals. Having consistent on-time payments over an extended period of time works more wonders for your credit score than merely taking out a loan and paying it off rather quickly. You may get tempted to do this to avoid paying further interest but keep the larger goal in mind. You're just gonna have to chalk that interest to the game in the name of improving your credit.

I hope that this can go without saying, but I'ma say it anyway: know the terms of your loan and exactly how it works. What's the interest rate? Is collateral needed? How much are your monthly payments? These are all things that you should know before taking any money from a lender.

Apply for a secured credit card

Secured credit cards are an excellent tool for building and improving credit. This type of credit card is called secured because a security deposit is required. This deposit serves as collateral, and will be used if you can't make your payments. If you owe more than your security deposit and the company decides to seize your deposit, you're still responsible for paying off the difference. You'll learn much more about secured credit cards in the next chapter.

Try becoming an authorized user

Being an authorized user gives you the ability to use someone else's credit card, but in your name. If you're an authorized user, then you aren't legally obligated to pay the credit card bill or associated debts. This responsibility falls on the primary account holder. Because of this, being an authorized user won't have a significant impact on improving your credit score. But, if you're just beginning to establish credit, it can definitely be beneficial.

It's important to ask if the credit card issuer reports authorized users to the credit bureaus. If they don't, this method is pointless because it won't help your score. Having a lender report you as an authorized user to the credit bureaus can slightly improve your credit score, but lenders care more about if you have been able to manage your own cards and accounts responsibly. This is why this isn't the preferred method for those trying to improve their credit score. It may be better suited as a means of having access to a particular credit card that you may not qualify for on your own merit.

REPAIRING YOUR CREDIT

Let's just go ahead and get this out of the way: there are no "Illuminati-type" of underground secrets to just magically repair your credit overnight. You can't just click your heels together three times and expect things to fall off of your credit report like a mechanical bull rider. It doesn't work like that, fam.

Any person or company that says that they can remove negative items from your credit report — even if the information is correct — is lying. There are two types of people in life that you should never trust: people who say that, and people who pour ketchup on their fries instead of dipping them.

If the information on your credit report is accurate, it's staying there. Luckily for a lot of people, though, the longest amount of time most negative items can stay on your credit report is limited to seven years and negative marks start becoming less impactful as time goes on. So, while negative marks may be of the same type, the more recent one will be weighed more heavily.

Before you can begin repairing your credit, it's important to know the different types of negative marks that can be on your credit report. They're not all created equal.

Late Payments

As we discussed earlier, payment history accounts for roughly 35% of your credit score. It's as critical as the mac and cheese during Thanksgiving.

Not only do companies want to get paid, but they also want to get paid on-time. Any time a payment is over 30 days late, it's fair game for a company to report it to the credit bureaus. Even if you pay the total amount owed on day 33, they can still choose to report it. Late payments are normally reported in 30-day increments (until it's finally sent off to collections). As you can imagine, the later the payment, the more it hurts your credit score.

Late payments will remain on your credit report for seven years from the original delinquency date. For example, let's say that you forgot to pay your phone bill and AT&T reports a 30-day late payment to the credit bureaus in April 2019. It will remain on your credit report until April 2026 — even if you make a payment after it's reported.

Charge-Offs and Collections

After a certain amount of time (usually 180 days past the due date) companies realize a debt is unlikely to be paid. When this happens, they will charge it off to have it taken off of their balance sheet. When a debt is charged off, that doesn't mean it disappears into thin air like Houdini and you're no longer responsible. It typically just means the original creditor sold it off to a "debt buyer," who then proceeds to try and collect the debt. Collection agencies usually buy these debts for pennies on the dollar like food stamps, in hopes of being able to convince you to pay them the amount owed. Once it's been sold off, you will then have a collection account. You can pay on a charge-off to prevent a collection account, but they're basically the same.

Collections and charge-offs remain on your credit report for seven years. Even if you pay the debt in full, it will remain on your credit report. The only difference is that it will show up as being paid off.

Usually, an account will only be sent to collections if there are no payments for four to six months. After this is when those annoying ass third-party collection agencies take over the efforts and start blowing up your phone. Before that happens, though, the company you owe will usually send a final notice about the debt. If possible, this is when it's in your best interest to try and negotiate a payment plan to avoid the debt from being sent off to a collection agency.

The amount that a collections account impacts your score varies widely, but generally speaking, the higher your score is prior to the collection, the more it will decrease. I know that seems odd, but the game is the game.

Back in the day, a paid collections account and an unpaid collections account would have the same effect on your credit score so it was pointless to pay it off because the damage had already been done. As time has progressed, FICO has updated their scoring model to basically "ignore" a collections account that had been paid off. So, if the company pulling your credit report uses one of the newer models, it could be in your best interest to pay off a collections account — depending on how long it's been on your report. If it's closer to the seven-year mark, then I wouldn't worry about it.

There are two important dates that you need to know when it comes to collections: the statute of limitations and the reporting limit. Don't let the similarity in the names confuse you. There's a big difference between them.

The statute of limitations, which can vary by state, represents the date when a debt collector can no longer use the court system to force you to pay your debt. Reaching the statute of limitations date doesn't mean the debt disappears and it doesn't stop the debt collector from contacting you — it just limits their legal power. It will still appear on your credit report.

Your reporting limit is generally seven years after the date of last activity, no matter your state. Given that most debt isn't charged off until after six months of missed payments, you can generally bet that your reporting limit will be seven years and six months after your last payment date.

Repossessions

When you take out an auto loan or lease a car, the car serves as collateral. If your loan ever goes into default, the car becomes fair game to be repossessed at any time that the lender sees fit.

Technically, a lender can consider your loan to be in a default status 30 days after the payment due date. However, the repossession process is a big hassle, so it's unlikely that a lender will consider you to be in default until you're at least 60 days late on your payment.

If you know for a fact that you will no longer be able to make payments and want to save yourself the humbling repossession experience, you can choose the voluntary repossession route — which is when you return the car back to the lender. A voluntary repossession does just as much harm to your credit score as a regular repossession (it's just less embarrassing), so don't do it with the sole intent of avoiding the damage to your credit.

If you're ever in the unfortunate situation of having your car repossessed, you'll be considered a high-risk borrower until the repossession disappears from your credit report. It will be tough to get financing for your next whip, and if you do get approved, your interest rate will be higher than cigarette prices in New York.

Not only will your credit score take a hit from the actual repossession being on there, but it would also have taken hits from the late and missed payments that caused the repossession in the first place. That's a Deontay Wilder one-two combo.

Foreclosure

In the event that you default on your mortgage loan (which is usually after 120 days of delinquency), your lender will start the foreclosure process. When this happens, the lender takes over ownership of your house. It takes a while for the process to complete, so you won't instantly be kicked out like Jazzy Jeff in Fresh Prince. You can definitely believe that it's going to show up on your credit report, though.

Needless to say, foreclosures are disastrous to your credit score. Some people have seen their score drop by 100 points.

The foreclosure will remain on your credit report for seven years after the original delinquency date — which is the due date of the first missed payment leading up to the foreclosure.

Bankruptcy

Bankruptcy is the legal process where a business or person declares that they are unable to pay their debts. Filing bankruptcy enables you to remove legal liability for some, or all of your debts.

There are multiple types of bankruptcy, but the two most common are Chapter 7 and Chapter 13.

Chapter 7 bankruptcy means that certain debts — like personal loans, credit cards, and medical bills — are entirely forgiven. With this forgiveness comes the agreement that a Trustee can sell certain assets that the person owns, and the money from the sales goes to the creditors that are owed. Certain state-specific assets, like your home, are exempt from being sold. If your home is near or in foreclosure, a Chapter 7 bankruptcy means the bank must immediately terminate foreclosure procedures.

Certain debts, however, are not forgiven with a Chapter 7 bankruptcy. Those include student loans, income taxes due, child support or alimony payments, and secured debts (debts backed by collateral).

With a Chapter 13 bankruptcy, your debts are not entirely forgiven. Instead, you're put on a payment plan that lasts anywhere between three to five years; with the mass majority of plans being five years. You'll pay a Trustee these payments and the Trustee will then pay the creditors that you owe. Unlike the Chapter 7, you won't have to sell your assets because you're paying on your debt with a payment plan.

There's no need to sugar coat it: filing for bankruptcy will hit your credit score with the force of a Kimbo Slice punch when he was fighting dudes in backyards on YouTube. It's not the end of the world by any means, but the consequences are undoubtedly real. While in your Chapter 13 bankruptcy payment plan, you can kiss any chance of getting financing for anything goodbye. After filing for a Chapter 7 bankruptcy, you can expect to be able to get financing for certain things not too long after the filing. However, certain life goals you may have will need to be put on hold for a few years — like if you had plans to get back into school and needed a loan, or if you wanted to refinance your mortgage for a better rate.

A Chapter 13 bankruptcy will be removed from your credit report seven years from the filing date, while a Chapter 7 bankruptcy will take ten years to be removed. The difference in time can be attributed to the fact that with a

Chapter 13 bankruptcy, you presumably made payments on the debt.

Again, if a negative item on your credit report is correct, there's no secret work-around to remove it. However, it's not farfetched for inaccurate information to be on your credit report. You'd be surprised at how often it happens. As a result, the first thing you should do when contacted about a debt is confirm that it actually belongs to you. Not every debt collector that hits you up is trying to collect on a legitimate debt — there are definitely scammers out there.

Debt validation

Debt collectors are required to send you a written validation of the debt that they're trying to collect. It should include who you owe, how much you owe, and a statement informing you that you have 30 days to dispute the debt. If they make the initial contact with you via phone, request that they contact you in writing. Do NOT give any information over the phone, until the debt and debt collector are 100% confirmed as legitimate.

If you have any ounce of doubt that the debt belongs to you, a good first step is to write a "debt verification letter." You have 30 days to dispute it, so don't loaf on the matter and get caught slippin'. If you send it within that timeframe, the debt collector must stop trying to collect the debt until the debt is verified as yours. After 30 days, the debt is assumed as valid. You can still send the debt verification letter; the collector just has the right to seek payment while verifying the debt.

You must physically send the debt collector your debt verification letter, it can't be done by email. When writing your letter, here are some key things that you will want to include:

- A statement clearly stating that you're requesting validation of the debt and **not** admitting to owing it.

- When you were contacted and by which method. For example,

"Your agency contacted me by your phone on February 28th."

- A statement asking who the creditor is, the amount owed, and the account number used by the creditor.

- A statement asking for verification that they have the authority to collect the debt.

- A statement asking for a copy of the last billing statement that they received by the original creditor.

There is an example of this letter in the appendix.

You will want to send this letter by **certified mail**, and request a return receipt so you will have exact details on when you sent the letter and when the collector received it. Although debt collectors are required by law to respond to debt verification letters, the only information they're required to provide you is the original creditor, the amount owed, and the name of the person who owes the debt. After that, they can resume their collection efforts.

If the debt collector fails to provide you with proof of the debt, all collection efforts must cease.

Credit report dispute

If you look at your credit report (which you should do regularly) and notice an error — whether it's an account that isn't yours, a missing account, or the wrong balance amount — you should write a credit dispute letter. Remember that not every lender reports to each of the three credit bureaus, so be sure to check all three reports.

When writing a debt dispute letter, be sure to send it to all three credit bureaus and any other related parties that may have reported the debt in question. It'll speed up the process, as they're both required to correct any inaccurate information. You can file disputes online with the credit bureaus, but sending a physical letter is usually more effective because they're not used to receiving them.

In the letter, you should include the following information:

- Your name, contact info, date of birth, and credit bureau account number.

- The credit bureau, department, and their address.

- A short description of the error. You don't have to write a novel; just tell them what's wrong and why it's wrong.

- A request to either delete or correct the information.

- A statement of the items that you're including with your letter.

Along with your letter, you're going to want to send any documentation that supports your dispute. After all, why the hell would they just take your word for it? That's about as likely as finding a Black person who smokes Marlboros instead of Newports. Be sure to send copies of the documents, and not the originals.

The envelope that you mail off should include:

- Your dispute letter.

- A copy of your credit report with the disputed item *circled* or **highlighted**.
- A copy of your government-issued ID.

- Proof of address (you can send a copy of a bill or something).

There is an example of this letter in the appendix.

Just like with debt verification letters, be sure to send it via **certified mail**, with a return receipt requested. I can't stress how important that is for documentation purposes. You should also keep copies of your dispute letter and the items enclosed.

The credit bureaus have to investigate the error within 30 days of receiving your dispute, and must notify you of their decision within 90 days (it usually doesn't take that long). Hopefully, they decide to remove the error, but sometimes they may ask for more information or reject the request outright.

If they reject your dispute and you know for a fact that it's an error, don't take no for an answer. Under NO circumstance should you pay for a debt that isn't yours. If you're in the business of doing that, feel free to holla at me; I have some student loans for you.

If you have negative items on your credit report that are legitimately yours, there are two 'hail mary' options that you can throw up. You can try writing a goodwill letter or a "pay-for-delete" letter.

Goodwill letter

It's not uncommon for people to be financially-responsible, have a good credit report, and then all of a sudden get hit with an uppercut from life. Perhaps a rough patch caused you to be late on a payment and now it's on your credit report.

If this is the case, then you may want to consider writing a goodwill letter. In a goodwill letter, you essentially ask the lender that reported the late payment to have the credit bureaus remove it from your credit report. Goodwill letters aren't an official 'strategy' and aren't broadcasted as an option by the credit bureaus, but it's definitely not the unlikeliest of things for someone to submit one. The chances of it working are about as good as finding a White man named Jamal, but, the fact that it's worked for some people should be enough reason to at least try it. The worst case is that they say "no" and you're in the same position that you started in. Shoot your shot!

A goodwill letter differs from a dispute in that you only reach out to the lender. You don't contact the credit bureaus. You're not claiming that the late payment is wrong. You're acknowledging your wrongs and asking for forgiveness. Unlike a dispute letter, you want to be intentionally personal, thoughtful, and genuine.

In the letter, you should include:

- Your personal information and account number.

- Date of the late payment.

- An explanation of the situation that caused the late payment.

- A statement explaining what has changed since then, to guarantee it won't happen again.

- A statement of how the late payment being on your credit report is hurting your ability to do something (i.e. qualify for an auto loan or mortgage).

- A statement specifically asking them for a "goodwill adjustment" instead of blatantly asking them to remove it. It also helps to send any supporting documents.

Like everything else credit report related, be sure to send it using *certified mail* with the return receipt request. Send it to the lender's address that is listed on your credit report.

If you're lucky, your lender will agree and have your credit report updated. If this happens, go to your nearest corner store or bodega immediately and buy some lottery tickets. No need to let that luck go to waste.

More than likely, though, they're going to say they can't legally remove correct information from your credit report (if they respond at all). If this happens, just charge it to the game — you had nothing to lose.

Save yourself the time and effort of sending a goodwill letter if:

- You don't have a good reason for the missed payment. "I forgot" won't suffice.

- You have multiple missed and/or late payments.

- Your credit utilization is currently high (it makes you seem riskier).

Pay-for-Delete letter

The "pay-for-delete" method is when a person asks a debt collector to erase a collection account in exchange for a payment. Paying on a collection account doesn't remove it from your credit report, so people try this method instead. Of course, debt collectors are required to provide accurate information to the credit bureaus, so this tactic has a few asterisks attached to it from an ethical standpoint. It's like paying your probation officer to get off of parole early.

Before sending a pay-for-delete letter, you should consider sending a debt verification letter first. If a debt collector can't verify that the debt is yours, then they can't list it on your credit report. It's worth trying.

When sending a pay-for-delete letter you're going to want to send it to the collection agency, **not** the original lender. Your letter should include:

- Your personal information and the account number.

- A specific amount that you're willing to pay as a settlement for the debt.

- A statement explicitly stating that the letter is **not** an acknowledgment or acceptance of the debt.

- A statement acknowledging the fact that their company has the ability to report the debt to the credit bureaus, as they deem necessary.

It doesn't make sense to go the pay-for-delete route if the collection account is old and due to be removed from your credit report within a couple of years. At that point, you're probably better off just waiting it out.

If you pull an Aaron Rodgers and the hail mary is successful, please be prepared to pay the full amount of the debt immediately. In fact, if you can't pay the full amount, you're not ready to send the letter. If the offer is accepted, they're going to want the payment provided to them quickly. You don't want the agreement revoked because you couldn't make the payment. Be sure to get the agreement in writing. A verbal agreement is like betting somebody without shaking their hand. You could get a verbal agreement, make the payment, and still not have the account removed from your credit report. Even worse, legally there'd be nothing you could do about it. That's humbling.

On the surface, the pay-for-delete tactic undermines the fundamental purpose of the entire credit reporting system. After all, the whole point is for your credit report to reflect your financial history accurately, right? As a result, I have my personal reservations about the use of this method.

HOWEVER...

I'm also a firm believer in playing the game and not letting the game play you. If the collection agency doesn't have a problem with it, then neither should you.

Your credit score can be a tool, or it can be a burden. Don't let it be a burden.

CHAPTER TWO

CREDIT CARDS

"Trickin', 'bout to run up the credit, max out the limit."
- FREDDIE GIBBS

Rumor has it that if you say "credit card" in the mirror three times, your parents will pop-up like Candyman, warning you of their dangers. When the average person hears credit card, the first things that come to mind are debt and stress. They're believed to go together like Batman and Robin, or Black male college athletes and White women.

The truth is that credit cards aren't nearly as bad as most people make them out to be. In fact, they can be a great thing. I'm not going to act like they're the best thing since sliced bread and the iPhone, because that might give off the impression that they're entirely harmless — which isn't true. However, most of the fear surrounding credit cards stems from the lack of understanding of how they work and believing the myths associated with them.

In today's society, knowing how to use credit cards responsibly is crucial to your financial well-being. This is especially true when it comes to building a good credit history. Although using a debit card may seem "safer," a credit card can be more beneficial.

CREDIT CARD INTEREST

One of the most misunderstood aspects of credit cards is the interest rate, and it's usually what discourages people from getting one. Most people understand the concept of paying interest on borrowed money, but not everyone understands just how credit card interest works.

To be fair, if you pay your balance in full each month, you'll never have to worry about interest and how it works. However, the vast majority of people will end up carrying over a balance on their credit card at some point during their lifetime and should be aware of how it works. That's just life. Everyone thinks that they're the exception until they're not.

For any purchases made during a billing cycle — which is typically around 30 days — you'll have a grace period (usually between 21 to 28 days) before your payment is due.

For example, if your credit card billing period is between March 26th and April 25th — with a due date of May 22nd — any purchases made within that time period will be interest-free as long as you pay the full balance by May 22nd. If you don't, you'll be charged interest. As a note, this period may be longer if you get an extended 0% interest introductory offer. Otherwise, this is how it works.

A common misconception is that interest is charged on the remaining balance after the payment due date. This is not true. If you don't pay your balance in-full by its due date, then interest will be charged based on your **average daily balance** during that billing period.

As an example, let's assume that your credit card balance is $1,000 for the first 10 days of a month, and then you make a $300 payment and carry a $700 balance for the next 10 days. After that, you make a $150 payment and carry a $550 balance through the remaining 10 days of the month. Your **average daily balance** would be $750. Refer to the calculation below for the breakdown:

$1,000 balance * 10 days = $10,000

$700 balance * 10 days = $7,000

$550 balance * 10 days = $5,500

The sum is $22,500. Divide this by 30 days and you will see that $750 is the average daily balance.

Just like it's important to know what your interest will be applied to, it is equally important to understand how that interest is calculated. Credit card purchases are subject to an interest rate called the **Annual Percentage Rate** ("APR"). The APR varies by card and by person, as it largely depends on certain factors such as your credit score. The higher your credit score, the lower your APR. The lower your credit score, the higher your APR. It's fairly straightforward. The "annual" in the name is semi-misleading, though, because although your APR is expressed in terms of a year, credit card companies calculate interest on a daily basis. This is called your **Daily Percentage Rate** ("DPR").

Your DPR can be calculated by dividing your APR by 365. If your APR is 15%, then your DPR will be 0.041096%. Before using your DPR in calculations, please be sure to convert the percentage to a decimal. In this case, the number becomes 0.00041096.

To figure out just how much interest you'll be charged, use the following formula: **Average Daily Balance * Daily Percentage Rate * Number of days in the billing period**.

Using the numbers from our example above, your formula would be:

$750 * 0.00041096 * 30 = $9.25 interest charged.

A credit card can either have a fixed APR or a variable APR. A fixed APR will always remain the same (except in extraordinary circumstances), while a variable APR will change over time. Be sure to check the terms and conditions of your credit card for specifics. Interest rates are often sprinkled in the fine print of credit card offers and disclosures like parsley on pasta.

There are five main types of APRs that you should be aware of:

Purchase APR: The standard interest rate charged as discussed earlier. It applies to any purchases made with your credit card, and is the one that you should be most familiar with and knowledgeable of.

Balance Transfer APR: The interest rate applied to the balance that's transferred from one credit card to another. Balance transfer cards will be discussed in an upcoming section.

Introductory APR: A temporary promotional interest rate that credit card companies will offer to encourage people to sign up. This APR is way lower than the card's regular APR, and it's not unusual for the promotional rate to be 0%.

Cash Advance APR: Although it's not recommended, you can, in fact, borrow money from your credit card company. This is referred to as a cash advance and it works like most traditional loans. The cash advance APR refers to the interest rate charged on the amount of borrowed cash.

Penalty APR: If your credit card payment gets to the point where it's more than 60 days past due (or if you violate other terms of the card), you could be hit with a penalty APR. This APR, as I'm sure you can guess, is higher than your regular APR. Much, much higher!

Again — and I can't stress this enough — if you pay your credit card balance in-full and on-time each month, you'll never have to worry about interest. You can tune it out like you do your spouse when they come home eager to tell you all about their day that you couldn't care less about.

Credit card companies consider people who never have to pay interest 'free-loaders' because they don't make any money off of them unless their cards have annual fees. People who continuously carry a balance from month-to-month are considered 'revolvers' because they're a consistent source of income for the credit card companies. They depend on people being revolvers because they're a significant source of income for them.

Be a freeloader, fam.

CREDIT CARD TYPES

There are four general types of credit cards that you will encounter, and they each have their respective pros and cons. We will cover all four in depth.

Secured

If you've never had a credit card before, or your current credit score is looking funny in the light, then a secured credit card may be right for you. They were made for that purpose and are easy to get approved for. The only jig, however, is that secured credit cards require a security deposit (usually equal to the credit card's spending limit). Your security deposit acts as collateral, in the event that you can't pay your debt. Credit card companies are much more willing to take a risk on someone with no credit or bad credit, if they know that they will at least receive some money-back when shit hits the fan and the debt isn't paid.

Secured credit cards work the same way as regular credit cards and come with the same perks and benefits. You'll still be responsible for making your payments on time and interest is calculated in the same manner.

Your security deposit will be returned to you if the account is ever closed or if you're lucky enough to have your card upgraded to unsecured.

Student

On the surface level, it can seem like student credit cards are meant for... well...students. They wouldn't be called that if not, right? In actuality, the "student" aspect of the credit card is misleading — kinda like Subway's '$5 footlongs' that you somehow always end up paying $8 for. Solely being a student isn't enough to qualify for one of these credit cards.

Student credit cards are essentially regular credit cards that are branded and marketed towards students. The marketing isn't as questionable as Six Flags using a creepy old White man as the face of their advertisements, but it's definitely misleading, nonetheless.

The application and vetting process is the same as a regular credit card, and unless you're at least 21 years old, you will need to be working full-time to get approved. Unless you took time off from school or had gap years after high school, you ironically won't qualify for a student credit card until you're damn near done with school. If you're neither 21 years old or have a full-time income, your best chance for getting approved is by having a co-signer. As a reminder, for most people, getting a co-signer isn't a likely outcome. Co-signing is a big task to ask any one — even family.

At this point, you're probably wondering why the hell they even call it a student credit card. The name was created back in the day when credit card companies were about as regulated as Bourbon Street in New Orleans. Credit card companies love college students like rent-a-cops love acting like they're Secret Service. When they see college students, they see a lot of years of interest payments ahead, and they see someone who may be able to rely on their parents if they get swipe-happy.

Credit card companies used to post-up on campuses as students moved-in, lure them in with free food (everybody loves free food) and t-shirts, and convince them to apply for their respective cards.

On one end, you had people who used the credit cards responsibly and were able to get an excellent financial head start. On the other end, a lot of people went wild and started off their adult lives in a financial hole. Imagine these people racing the length of a football field. People who used their card responsibly essentially started at the 30-yard line, and people who went wild started at the goal line. If you were a minority that went wild, you basically started from the locker room.

As time has progressed, the laws have changed to protect vulnerable consumers — like young people who could quickly rack up debt from mismanaging their credit card — by tightening up the criteria for qualifying for a credit card.

Student credit cards do occasionally offer perks that are catered to current students. These could include discounts on various streaming services, cash back for good grades, and other enticing introductory offers.

When choosing a student credit card, here are some things to look for:

• No annual fees. As a student, you're already strapped for cash, so there's no need to get a credit card with an annual fee. Besides, the selection of cards without an annual fee is as plentiful as adlibs in a Migos song.

• No foreign transaction fees. You never know when you may find yourself in Cancun for spring break doing things you pray don't end up on the internet. Perhaps, you will get the opportunity to study abroad in Europe, where you spend more time drinking wine than actually studying. In the spirit of cutting unnecessary expenses – so you can use that extra money partying, of course – you're going to want a credit card with no foreign transaction fees. If you know for a fact that you'll be abroad in the future, be especially diligent in making sure your card doesn't have these fees.

• Rewards. There are too many student cards that include lucrative perks to settle for a bottom-shelf card that won't compensate you for giving them your business. If you're going to get a credit card, why not get one with benefits? As a note, any card with rewards will have higher interest

rates. Keep this in mind when determining the overall value of the card.

Balance Transfer

Sometimes life comes at you fast. You may suddenly lose your job, incur unexpected medical expenses, or you may even go through a depressive episode and decide binge-shopping online is the best way to cope. Whatever the case, sometimes you blink twice and your credit card balance is higher than somebody who took a second weed edible because they didn't think the first one was working. Sometimes this debt is so high that it could take months or years to pay off the balance. Add interest rates into the equation, and this could be costlier than you can imagine.

Balance transfer credit cards can help you get out of debt faster by saving you money on interest. They allow you to transfer your outstanding balance from one credit card (or multiple credit cards) to another credit card and gives you an extended period where you pay minimal interest. This allows you to focus on paying on the principal of the debt, which cuts the time it takes to pay it off.

Let's say you have two credit cards: one with a $1,500 balance and 15% APR, and one with a $2,000 balance and 20% APR. Instead of paying the respective APR on both cards, you could transfer these two balances to a balance transfer card that would then have a $3,500 balance with a 0% (or very low percentage) introductory APR for a given period of time. It's generally around 12 months.

Now, if you're thinking it sounds too good to be true, then you're kinda right. Balance transfer cards are not for everyone. I repeat: balance transfer cards are not for everyone.

Before deciding if you should go this route, ask yourself a few questions:

- Are your current interest rates making it unreasonably hard to repay your debt?

- Do you carry balances from month-to-month on your current credit card(s)?

- Do you have a serious strategy for paying down your debt during the introductory period of your balance transfer credit card?

If you answered yes to all three of these questions, then a balance transfer card may be right for you. Of the three, the last question is the most important. Without a plan, choosing to go with a balance transfer credit card is like putting on cologne while you're musty — it may mask the problem for a little bit, but it doesn't solve the real issue. Understand what got you into that debt to begin with. If you don't address the root-cause, you're hustlin' backwards.

If after going through the mental checklist you decide that a balance transfer card is right for you, there are a few things to be aware of. The first being that transferring your balance comes with a fee. This fee generally ranges between 3 - 5% of the total balance transferred. Depending on how much you plan on transferring, this amount could be enough to make you say to hell with transferring your balance.

Here are the recommended steps for transferring your balance(s):

1) **Review and write down your current credit card balances and interest rates**. If you don't know this information, then chances are you're not informed enough to know if you need a balance transfer card.

2) **Get your most recent credit score, so you'll know which credit cards you can realistically get approved for.** There's no need to increase the number of inquiries on your credit report by applying for credit cards you stand no chance of being approved for. Stay in your lane, fam. Your credit score will thank you.

3) **Research and apply for a card with a 0% (or very low) introductory APR.** There's a lot of balance transfer cards out there, and none are necessarily "better" than the rest. It really depends on what's right for you and your respective financial situation. Here are some things to consider when choosing a card to apply for:

- How much is the annual fee?
- What is the APR and how long is the introductory promotional period?
- What is the balance transfer fee?
- What is the transfer limit (if any)?

4) **Apply.** Usually, during the application process, credit card companies will ask you to provide information about your current credit cards. This information could include the balance owed. If approved, you will either be able to transfer all or a portion of your existing credit card balances; it all depends on the credit limit that you're approved for.

You could have two balances of $2,000 and $1,500 and only get approved for a $3,000 credit limit on the balance transfer card. In this case, you'd still have to keep $500 on one of your old cards. In the event that you're not approved for a credit limit that covers all your existing debt, think long and hard about if you still want to go through with the transfer. You'll still save money on interest on the transferred amount, but you'll lose the simplification benefit of having your debt in one place.

You may be wondering how a balance transfer credit card impacts your credit score. Depending on your current financial situation, it will affect it in one of two ways. No matter what, your credit score will momentarily drop by a few points when you apply for the card, as it does with any hard inquiry. But, depending on the credit limit that you're approved for, you could instantly improve your credit utilization.

For example, if you maxed out your current cards at $2,000 and $1,500 and get approved for a balance transfer card with a credit limit of $5,000, your credit utilization will drop from 100% to 41% ($3,500 used out of $8,500). This is still higher than preferred, but a notable improvement nonetheless.

Even after you get approved and transfer your balances to the new credit card, it's crucial that you do not close out your old cards. Since the length of your credit history is an important aspect of your credit score, you don't want to close an account and risk shortening this time. Closing out a card will also decrease the amount of available credit you have, consequently increasing your credit utilization. Both of which will have a negative impact on your credit score.

Overall, when it comes to balance transfer credit cards and whether or not they're right for you, you need to keep it real with yourself. Understand and address the underlying factor(s) that got you into the debt in the first place. Don't try to use a balance transfer credit card as a quick fix because you'll usually end up in a worse situation than before. It happens every day, B.

Reward

Reward credit cards allow you to earn incentives when you make purchases with your credit card. This type of credit card is perfect for you, if you use your credit card regularly and pay off your entire balance each month. They're lucrative because they compensate you for using your credit card throughout your daily life.

Each card usually focuses on a specific reward type — cash back, flight miles, or hotel points. As with most things in life, if it sounds too good to be true, it probably is.

Not only do they require that you have better-than-average credit, but reward credit cards are also known for having high annual fees and APRs compared to other card types. This is why I emphasized that these are perfect for people who pay their bill in full each month. If you don't have to worry about paying interest, then the rewards are essentially free (excluding the annual fee). There's no need for all those rewards, if you're gonna be paying more in interest than the rewards are worth. That's hustlin' backwards, fam.

Cash back

Cash back credit cards allow you to earn cash rewards for your purchases. It's like getting paid to spend money. The cash rewards are either paid via statement credit, direct deposit, or check. Most of the time, you'll be able to choose which method you prefer. The complexity of the cash back rewards varies widely depending on the card.

The overwhelming majority of cash back cards will offer 1% cash back for purchases made. This is a cash back card in its simplest form. You can easily find 1% cash back credit cards that don't come with any catches, limitations, or hidden conditions. They're as straightforward as anything in the finance world: spend x amount, get 1% of x amount back in cash rewards. It's not rocket science.

However, cards that offer more than 1% back in rewards almost always have a catch to them. Cash back programs can be expensive for credit card companies, so you know that they had to create some stipulations that help them avoid being completely assed out. That's just how the game goes. The conditions and/or limitations normally aren't extreme and most won't inconvenience you, but it's important to read the terms and conditions of the rewards when more than 1% in cash back rewards is offered.

You can also find cards that offer flat rate cash back bonuses in particular categories — with gas, groceries, and restaurants being the most common — annually. The amount could be the standard 1%, or it could be as high as 6%. Be cognizant, though, that the higher the cash back percentage, the more likely it is that there's a cap on how much you can spend. For example, credit card ABC may offer 5% cash back on grocery store purchases, but only up to $5,000 per year in purchases. After you've spent $5,000 at grocery stores that year, your rewards will usually drop down to the standard 1%. Make sure you're aware if this is the case, so that you're not misled on your reward potential.

Another important item to note is that these cards don't offer rewards for all purchases of gas and groceries. They offer rewards for purchases of gas at gas stations and purchases at grocery stores — there's a big difference between the two.

You can buy gas and groceries at Walmart, but you won't receive any rewards because it's neither a gas station nor a grocery store (even though they sell both). Wording matters, and as I'm sure you can imagine, credit card companies aren't the most transparent and explanatory with their terms and conditions. It'd be humbling to be buying all your groceries at Sam's Club or Costco, only to find out that you didn't receive any rewards because the store didn't qualify.

Another type of cash back rewards card that you're likely to run into are the ones that offer a flat 5% cash back on rotating categories that change every three months. It could be gas, groceries, or even Amazon.com purchases. You never know.

You can expect to earn 1% cash back on all purchases outside of the rotating category. You can also expect to see a spending cap (normally $1,500) on the rotating category. If your current quarterly rewards category is Amazon.com, for example, you can't just spend $10,000 on their website and expect to get back $500 ($10,000 * 5%) back in rewards. Unfortunately, it doesn't work like that, fam. You'd receive 5% cash back on the first $1,500 and then 1% cash back on the remaining $8,500, totaling $160 in total rewards. Here's the math:

$10,000 total spent: ($1,500 * 5% = $75) + ($8,500 * 1% = $85) = $160.

An important thing to make note of, when dealing with credit cards with rotating reward categories, is that you have to activate the respective bonus category every quarter. Let me write that again for emphasis: you have to activate the respective bonus category every quarter.

Forgetting to do it can cause you to lose out on a good amount of cash back. Missing out on that "free" money will have you mad enough to toss your credit card into the nearest lake or ocean, like a frisbee.

You can usually activate the category a couple of weeks before the quarter begins. If you know that you have the memory of a pothead, just do yourself a favor and set a reminder on your phone. You can literally just pick up your iPhone and say, "Hey Siri, remind me to set my quarterly credit card category on [insert whatever date here]." Once you set your category for the upcoming quarter, set another reminder for the next quarter. Rinse and repeat. Start using your iPhone for something more useful than scrolling your Twitter timeline and laughing at old Vine videos.

Before deciding which cash back credit card to go with, it's important to know your spending habits and what you will use the card for. If you order takeout for dinner every evening, a card that offers high cash back at grocery stores wouldn't be of much value to you. Similarly, if you live in that concrete jungle that we call New York City and take the subway everywhere, a card that offers high cash back on gas at gas stations would be about as useful as using a fork to eat soup.

Be sure to align the credit card you choose with your spending habits and lifestyle. If not, you may spend more in annual fees than you receive in rewards. Don't hustle backwards.

Once you find a card that suits your lifestyle and begin to use it responsibly, it can be a significant perk to have. After all, who would turn down free money?

Travel

If traveling is a part of your lifestyle or something you hope to incorporate into your lifestyle soon, then a travel rewards credit card could be perfect for you. These cards allow you to earn airline miles whenever you make purchases. It's the same principle as cash back rewards, except airline miles are the reward instead of cash. Travel credit cards usually fall into one of two categories: generic or airline-specific.

With generic airline miles cards, your reward points can be redeemed through numerous airlines and travel agencies. If you don't have a go-to airline or you're not a part of any frequent flier program, these types of cards are great options for you. You'll have the flexibility to redeem your miles with whatever airline best accommodates your trip. The downside, however, is that even though you'll receive points for purchases, you won't receive any additional points for flying.

On the other hand, Airline-specific cards are co-branded with major airlines. This is perfect if you do have a go-to airline and/or are a part of a frequent flier program. Not only will you acquire points from your purchases, chances are that you'll also earn points when you fly. It's a win-win.

Aside from the points earned, a lot of co-branded airline credit cards offer perks such as free checked bags, priority boarding, access to their airport lounges, and more.

Travel credit cards are also notorious for offering lucrative sign-up bonuses. Often times, these bonuses offer tens of thousands of points or miles if you spend a certain amount within a given time period of opening the account. For example, Card XYZ may offer 30,000 bonus miles if you spend $5,000 within the first three months of opening the account. For some people, this is no big deal because they would have spent that much during that time period regardless. For others, this isn't reasonable with their current budget and spending habits — which is perfectly fine. Never go out of your way to make sure that you spend a certain amount just for the introductory reward bonus. Rarely will this work out in your favor. It usually just ends with people having a balance that they can't pay off, which subsequently acquires a good chunk of interest. If you wouldn't usually spend that much in that given timeframe, just chalk it up to the game, fam. Don't go from an Applebee's 2 for $20 budget to a Ruth's Chris budget overnight. It's not worth it.

The smart way to achieve the spending amount during the bonus window is to determine how much money you would spend on your bills during the three-month window. I have often reached these spending limits easily when I've added my credit card as the primary payment method for my bills. Auto-pay is a great feature for recurring payments. Additionally, you may want to check with your apartment to see if you can pay your rent with credit cards. Find ways to make this promotion work for you, without making unnecessary large-ticket item purchases.

Also, be aware that the promotional period begins when you get approved for the credit card, not when you receive or activate the card. So, if you got approved on January 1st but didn't activate your card until January 15th, you would still be considered two weeks into the promotional period. Don't get caught slippin' and miss your spend deadline because you misinterpreted your timeframe.

As with every type of credit card, travel cards have cons to go along with their benefits. For starters, you will need a good credit score to be approved for one. If your credit score is sub-par, save yourself the hard inquiry and credit score hit and don't even bother applying.

Depending on the airline, there may be a cap on the number of miles you can earn annually, and unused miles may expire after a certain amount of time. This varies by card so be sure to double-check. Another catch (because there's always a catch, right?) is that travel credit cards usually come with high ass annual fees. These fees won't mean much, though, if you use the card responsibly and take full advantage of the perks. For example, if a credit card has a $100 annual fee but offers free checked bags (which are typically $25 - $30), and you fly at least four times per year, the annual fee is worth it because it pays for itself.

Hotel

Just like with flying, there are rewards to be earned that can be put towards your hotel stays. And just as airlines have co-branded credit cards, hotel chains do as well. Perks include, but are not limited to, free hotel nights, upgraded room accommodations, and various other offerings that can enhance your stay at their respective hotels. The more general, all-purpose rewards cards, can be used to earn credit that can be utilized for other travel-related things such as rental cars.

As a best practice, you should identify at least one hotel chain and airline that you prefer to do business with. By remaining loyal, you will maximize your reward potential and attain status that makes your experience worthwhile. It's important to understand the psychology behind the introductory offers. The intent is to get the consumer used to swiping the card, in an attempt to receive the reward. Unknowingly, the consumer has developed a habit of swiping the card frequently. Credit card companies benefit from this behavior, as this keeps the consumer tied to unnecessary debt.

MYTHS

Columbus "discovered" America. Lightning never strikes the same place twice. Stevie Wonder is blind. What do all three of these things have in common? They're all myths.

Like these myths, credit card myths, have been repeated to the point where a disturbing number of people now believe them to be true. This is unfortunate. Nowadays, people are so gullible that they will believe anything on the internet with good grammar and proper punctuation. However, unlike most myths you hear, believing certain credit card myths can have real consequences and cause people to make uninformed decisions. I'm sure that I don't have to tell you that this is not a good thing, but I'm gonna do it anyway: that's not a good thing.

Here are the most common credit myths that you should stop believing immediately:

1) You need to carry a balance on your credit card to improve your credit.

This is undoubtedly one of the biggest credit card myths floating around. It's just not true. As I've expressed on numerous occasions, your credit utilization accounts for 30% of your credit score and keeping your utilization low — ideally below 30% — is one of the best ways to improve your credit score. Not only will carrying a balance increase your credit utilization, but it's also the quickest way to have interest charges sneak up on you like a thief in the night. If you're worried about your account not being active (which you probably shouldn't be), pay a single bill with the card each month and then pay the balance off immediately. Your card will remain active, and you won't have to worry about any interest.

2) Having too many credit cards hurts your credit score.

Your credit score is not affected by how many credit cards you have. What's more important is the balances you have on your credit cards. One benefit of having multiple cards is that it increases your total amount of available credit and consequently lowers your credit utilization. As long as you're spending responsibly and paying your full balances each month, you can have enough credit cards to build a life-size replica of the Taj Mahal if you choose. (That's an exaggeration, of course, but you get my point).

3) You should avoid credit cards with annual fees.

Trust me when I say that you're not the only person walking on God's green earth that hates paying fees. We all hate it, fam. However, some annual fees are worth paying because the benefits and perks from the credit card outweigh the annual fee that you'll pay. This isn't to say that all annual fees are worth it, but you can definitely justify some.

Typically, the higher the annual fee, the more lucrative the perks are. Don't avoid a credit card solely based on the annual fee if you can reasonably reap more in benefits than you pay out. However, If the rewards don't add up to the fee, leave it be. For example, if a card with a $50 annual fee offers 1% cash back, it wouldn't make sense to have it if you don't plan on spending at least $5,000 on it that year because you'll end up paying more in fees than you'll receive in rewards.

4) Closing out a credit card will help you.

It's not uncommon for someone to get the urge to close out one of their credit cards. Sometimes it's because they've recently gotten out of debt and they don't want to give themselves a chance to get back into it. Other times, it's because the credit card is just sitting around collecting dust and they're not using it. Either way, you should steer away from closing out a credit card, regardless of the circumstances.

There are two main reasons for this. For one, when you close a credit card you automatically lower the amount of available credit you have, which consequently increases your credit utilization and hurts your credit score. Secondly, you risk shortening your credit history when you close an old account. Because the length of your credit history is factored into your credit score, this will negatively affect it. Especially if the credit card was the first account on your credit report.

While people will close a credit card with the intent of practicing good financial habits, they ironically end up hurting their credit score by doing it. Don't make that mistake.

5) Your minimum spend timeclock begins once you activate your card.

As we discussed earlier with rewards credit cards, often times these cards will come with introductory bonuses that you'll receive if you spend a certain amount of money within a specific timeframe. I again want to note that the timeclock for these promotions starts when you get approved for the card, not when you receive or activate the card. It seems simple, but you'd be surprised how many people miss out on the bonuses because they misjudged just how much time they had to make purchases and qualify for it. Don't fall victim.

MISTAKES TO AVOID

Now that we've covered myths associated with credit cards, let's cover some common mistakes that you should avoid:

- Paying only the minimum amount due. The most common mistake people make with credit cards is just paying the minimum amount due. That's the main ingredient in the credit card debt recipe. When the dreadful time comes when you have to pay your bill, you'll notice a "minimum payment due" amount listed (usually between $25 and $35). Paying only the minimum amount due doesn't do much for you, except ensure that you don't have any late fees or missed payment infractions on your credit report. While both of those are important, habitually only paying the minimum amount due will leave you paying more in interest than you'd like to imagine. As previously stated, paying off the statement amount in-full each month ensures that you pay no interest. This is almost like borrowing money for free.

- Maxing out your credit card. This may seem obvious, but trust me, it happens every day, dawg. Aside from an emergency, your credit card limit should not be a challenge to spend up to that amount. Having 100% credit utilization will drop your credit score quicker than the speed of the shoe your grandma used to throw at you when you talked back to her growing up. Even if you plan to pay-off the entire balance at the due date, having a maxed-out credit card throughout the billing cycle will still hurt you because it's likely that your credit card company will have reported your balance to the credit bureaus during that time period.

- Applying for too many credit cards at once. As you know, every time you apply for a credit card your credit score takes a small hit for a short period of time, due to the hard inquiry. Applying for several cards in a short time frame is not only a bad idea because your credit score will lower with each hard inquiry, but it's also a red flag to lenders and will drastically reduce your approval chances. From a lender's perspective, applying for multiple lines of credit within a short time-frame is a sign that you desperately need access to credit. This, more often than not, makes you appear a lot riskier than the average consumer. Be sure to space out your applications and only apply for credit cards as you need them; not just for the sake of getting a new one. If you're thinking about getting another credit card to increase your amount of available credit, try asking for a credit line increase on your current credit card(s) instead.

CHAPTER THREE

INVESTING

"I'ma get them commas and invest."
—GUNNA

When the average person thinks of an investor, they often get the wrong impression. They picture somebody sitting around reading *The Wall Street Journal* and watching Bloomberg TV all day. They imagine the stock exchange looking like scenes from *The Wolf of Wall Street*. And, unfortunately, they believe that you have to be tremendously smart or rich to invest. The truth is that none of those have to be true. If you've watched the news in the last few years, I'm sure you've heard about just how much the stock market has been boomin'. The real question, however, is who exactly is benefitting from the boom? Only 54% of Americans currently invest in stocks (including through retirement plans), and for Black folks, this number sits even lower at only 36%.

It's no secret that stocks are a great tool for creating and growing wealth. History has showed us this time and time again. So, considering the benefits of investing, why do minorities shy away from the stock market? Part of this has to do with familiarity (or lack thereof), part of it is psychological, and part of it is a lack of resources. Considering older generations were more focused on preserving the little bit of money they had, investing – especially in the stock market – wasn't a conversation many of us had growing up.

Even minorities who have the "extra" money avoid the stock market like the plague. This is especially true for Black folks. Historically, when we invest, we tend to focus on fixed investments that are "low-risk" and provide very low returns – like real estate. Prior to the U.S. housing bust, over 60% of Black folks thought real estate was a better investment than stocks. In the past decade, the median house price has increased by 17%. During that same time period, the S&P 500 (which consists of the 500 largest American companies) increased by 125%. Not only does this contribute to the wealth gap because White people are more likely to invest in the stock market (thus receiving higher returns), but it also proved costly during the housing bust because so much of Black family wealth was tied up in housing.

The first time I looked into investing, it took all of 10 minutes before I was closing my laptop and hopping back on NBA 2K. There's so much information out there that it can be overwhelming for someone who's looking to get started. So much so that people rather say to hell with investing than to take the time to learn how it works. To a lot of people, learning about investing and taking an Ambien are the same thing.

With all the investment lingo and terms out there, it's easy to get lost in the sauce. If you're new to investing, focus on the basics and get a solid foundation before worrying about more complex things. I can promise you that Michael Jordan learned how to do a layup before he was gliding from the free throw line.

When it comes to investing, an important term for you to familiarize yourself with is **security**. Not to be confused with the 6'4", 250 pound bouncer at your local club that thinks he's guarding the Gates of Heaven. Simply put, securities are financial assets that have value and can be traded.

Stocks and bonds are two types of securities, but are not the only securities. All securities fall into one of two categories: equity or debt.

Stocks are equity securities because they represent ownership. When you buy a stock, you're buying ownership of a company. Bonds are debt securities because they represent loans. When you buy a bond, you're loaning money to the institution that issued it.

BUYING

There are four main ways to buy and sell securities: through a brokerage company, through banks, through individual investors, or directly from the company that issues them. Rarely (if ever) will you use the last three options.

Brokerage company

Think of brokerage companies as middlemen. If you want to buy securities, they'll go find a seller; if you want to sell securities, they'll go find a buyer. And in true middleman fashion, they charge a fee for doing it.

Back in the day, if you wanted to place a trade, you'd have to call up your stockbroker and place an order over the phone like Chinese take-out. As with seemingly everything in life except voting, brokerage companies have gone digital. Nowadays, you can execute a trade in a few simple clicks.

To get started, you simply open a brokerage account, deposit money into the brokerage account from your bank account, and then use your brokerage account to buy the securities that you want.

These accounts are taxable, so you can expect to pay taxes on the interest you earn and the profit you make from selling a security. If you buy a stock for $20 and sell it for $25, you will owe taxes on $5. You know Uncle Sam always gotta get his.

There are many brokerage companies that you can choose from, and finding one that works for all investors is damn near impossible. Here are some things to consider before deciding on a broker:

1) Know what you need.

More than anything, picking the right broker involves identifying your investing goals and level of expertise.

If you're new to investing, things like educational resources, excellent customer service, and a user-friendly platform can make a world of difference. Those things may not matter to a more advanced investor who may be more concerned about advanced tools and other complicated things that the average person couldn't care less about.

- Educational resources

Many brokers offer educational content that investors of all expertise can benefit from, but it can be especially helpful to beginners. From free courses, to webinars, to explanation videos, there's no shortage of offerings. Choose a broker that not only lets you place trades, but also provides you with the resources you need to make informed decisions. It's like having a gym that provides workouts and nutrition tips, instead of just providing a physical building with weights and treadmills.

- Customer service

Just like you can count on somebody asking for a piece when you pull out a pack of gum in public, you can also count on needing assistance from customer support at some point. That's just the nature of the game. If you're a person who knows you'd prefer to talk to someone face-to-face, choosing a broker that has physical locations close to you would be a priority. If you're cool with email or phone support, this wouldn't matter. Either way, always check to see when the support is available. If you work from 9am to 5pm Monday through Friday, choosing a broker that only offers support from 9am to 5pm Monday through Friday would be as beneficial as ski lessons in Africa.

- User-friendly platform

Investing is already confusing enough; the last thing you want to do is choose a platform that's hard to use. That's adding insult to injury. Imagine doing your research and finally deciding on which assets you want to buy – only to go to your broker's platform and not even know how to place a trade. That's like putting on your best outfit to go out and not getting in the club because you got lost on the way there. If you don't feel comfortable navigating the platform, don't use it.

2) Figure out the fees.

While fees aren't necessarily the most important factor when picking a brokerage company, they're a close second. You're investing to make money. Spending a lot of what you make on fees defeats the purpose.

If you plan to buy and sell stocks frequently, choosing a broker with high commission fees would be hustlin' backwards. Those per-trade fees add up, and will eat away your returns like Pac-Man. Unless you're using a commission-free platform, you can expect to pay between $5 and $7 per trade.

If you plan to be more passive and hold on to stocks for a while, you could justify a higher commission fee for other benefits because you won't be trading often. Your bigger concern would be avoiding a broker with a high annual or monthly fee.

In addition to any fees, you should know if the broker requires a minimum deposit to open an account. It's possible to find brokers that don't, but many do, so double-check. It doesn't matter how much you love a broker, or how good of a fit it is if you can't afford the minimum deposit. You're basically window-shopping. Some minimum deposits can be as "low" as $500, and some can be as high as $10,000.

3) Understand the investment options.

Most brokers offer the same type of investments, but this isn't always the case. While some seemingly offer any asset under the sun, some may have limited options (like only stocks). Even if you don't want to invest in a particular type of asset now doesn't mean you won't want to later on down the road.

4) Consider the promotions.

By no means do you want a promotion to be the only reason that you choose a broker. Nothing about that is smart. However, if you're entirely indifferent between two brokers, a promotion could be the deciding factor.

There are plenty of resources online that can help you compare brokers, so there's no reason to make an uninformed decision. Know your financial situation and goals, and choose the one that's right for you.

Banks

You won't be able to buy stocks from a bank, but most of them do offer bonds. Banks are convenient because you can typically just walk in and buy them on the spot. But, the downside is that you're limited to whatever they offer — which is usually much less than a brokerage company's selection.

From another person

This method is very uncommon. Transferring ownership from one person to another sounds simple, but it's not as easy as it seems. You have to request a physical stock certificate (the document that certifies ownership of stock), sign it over to the new owner, and then send it back to the company so that they can register it under the new owner's name. It's usually not worth the hassle.

Directly from the company

Like buying directly from a person, this method is uncommon and the average investor will never use this approach. All companies don't offer this option, but one advantage to this method is that you get to bypass the broker fees.

All things considered, your best option is to go through a brokerage company. It's your one-stop-shop for investing.

STOCKS

As I mentioned earlier, stocks are a type of equity security. If you buy shares in Nike, you now own a percentage of Nike. That's why companies on the stock market are considered "public companies" — anyone can buy a part of ownership.

Although they're sometimes used interchangeably, the distinction between "stocks" and "shares" is that stock is a broad term that describes ownership in one or more companies, while shares refers to ownership in a specific company.

All fancy terminology aside, stocks exist for one underlying reason: companies need money, and luckily for them, people have money they're willing to give for a chance at making more money. It's a match made in heaven — kinda like Black folks and Hennessy, or White girls and pumpkin spice lattes.

HOW STOCKS WORK

To understand how stocks work, let's imagine that you live in Los Angeles, want to open up your own marijuana dispensary and need $100,000 to get started. You incorporate your company, divide it into 1,000 shares, and sell them at $100 each (giving you the $100,000 you need).

If your business profited $20,000 during the year, you would take that amount and divide it by the 1,000 shares, resulting in $20 **earnings per**

share ("EPS"). The concept of EPS is critical in investing.

Now, you have to decide what to do with that profit. You can choose to re-invest some (or all) of the profit back into the company for business purposes, or you can give some of the profit back to shareholders in the form of a **dividend** — which is just the fancy name given to the money companies pay to their shareholders. Out of the $20 EPS, you may decide to pay out a $5 dividend to shareholders and re-invest the other $15.

The dividend amount varies by company, and some companies — especially newer ones — won't pay out any dividend because they need the money to continue growing. Once a company gets to a certain size, their growth potential slows, and they typically become more lenient with their dividends.

Dividends — which are paid every three months to your bank account, brokerage account, or in the form of additional shares that are re-invested — represent one of two primary ways that you can make money from stocks. The other way is through an increase in the value of a share.

Let's assume your business has been boomin' and is now valued at $500,000. Each one of those 1,000 shares you originally created is now worth $500 instead of $100. If you owned one share and sold it, the $400 you profited would be considered a **capital gain**.

The money earned from capital gains plus dividend payouts is considered the stock's total return.

The total return is an aspect of investing that is commonly overlooked by beginners. While a change in the price of a stock is notable, it doesn't give the full picture on whether or not an investment is good or bad. Looking at the total return is much more appropriate.

If you own a stock for a while and the price only changes by a few percentages (if at all), this may lead you to believe that it was a bad investment. This isn't necessarily the case. Dividends usually make up the bulk of a stock's total return; judging an investment without considering them is like watching the old Cleveland Cavaliers and judging how good they were in a game when LeBron wasn't playing. If you plan to hold on to a stock for a while, there's no real reason to stress about the constant changes in its price if those dividend payments are hitting your account regularly.

You can find your total return percentage by adding the amount you've earned in dividends to the amount earned from capital gains, and dividing it by how much you originally bought the stock for.

Let's say you bought $20,000 worth of Nike shares and five years later, sold those same shares for $25,000. If you earned $1,000 in dividends during those five years, you'd find your total return by doing the following:

$25,000 + $1,000 = $26,000

$26,000 / $20,000 = 1.3

1.3 - (1.0) = 0.3 or **30% total return.**

The 1.0 you subtract out is the original $20,000 (called the principal) that you invested.

Deciding whether it was a good investment depends on your own definition of "good" and how long the investment was held. If you got a 10% return in a year, that may be considered good. If it took you a decade to get a 10% return, yuck.

If you're hopping into the stock investing game with intentions of getting rich strictly from capital gains, you're in for some frustrating times.

STOCK MARKET

Think of the stock market as one big ass auction. On one end, you have parties that want to sell stocks. On the other end, you have parties that want to buy stocks.

I intentionally use the term parties because it could be people, corporations, or governments doing the buying or selling.

This auction-like dynamic is what causes a stock's price to rise and fall. If there are more buyers than sellers of a stock, its price will increase. If there are more sellers than buyers, its price will drop. It's supply and demand.

It's not necessarily a company's actions that influence its stock price; it's how investors react to those actions.

FUNDS

Other than buying shares in individual companies, a common way to invest is through funds. Funds are a collection of securities assembled into one entity, allowing you to invest into a group of companies all at once.

The three broad types of funds you need to know are: mutual funds, index funds, and exchange-traded funds ("ETFs").

Mutual funds

Think of a mutual fund as an Easter basket. Just like an Easter basket has a variety of items in it, a mutual fund consists of a variety of securities – including stocks, bonds, and other assets.

It's no secret that it's important to have a diversified portfolio in investing. The problem is that it takes a lot of time and effort to do that. Imagine having to drive to a different store for every single item in the Easter basket.

That's where mutual funds come into play. Instead of you having to do the work, a professional puts the fund together and manages it for you. Imagine sending your lil' cousin on errands to get the items for the Easter basket (and then putting it together for you). Although you could probably strong-arm your lil' cousin into doing it for free, you should be smart enough to know it doesn't work like that in the finance world.

The fee charged by funds – regardless of the type – is referred to as the **expense ratio.** It's expressed as a percentage of your investments and is charged annually. Since professionals actively manage mutual funds, their expense ratios are usually noticeably higher than index funds or ETFs. It's not uncommon for a mutual fund to have an expense ratio of 1% or more. At that rate, you'd pay $10 in fees for every $1,000 you have invested.

Index funds

An index fund is a type of mutual fund.

To understand index funds, you have to understand what an index is. An index is a hypothetical collection of assets grouped based on certain criteria. Some indexes may only have companies of a particular industry (like tech or agricultural), and some may be grouped by the size of the companies. For example, the most famous index, the S&P 500, is made up of the 500 largest American companies. There are even indexes that only consist of companies that are deemed "socially responsible." The list goes on.

An index fund is the actual fund that's put together to mirror a particular index. When you invest into an S&P 500 index fund, you're technically not investing in the S&P 500; you're investing in a fund that is made up of the companies in the S&P 500.

It's like having an Easter basket, but the only items in there have to meet a certain criteria – like only chocolate candy, or items made locally.

When you buy an index fund, your money isn't split evenly between all of the companies in the fund. It's divided based on the companies' **market capitalization** — which is found by multiplying their share price by the number of shares they've issued. For example, a company that's issued 1,000,000 shares and has a current share price of $25 would have a market capitalization of $25,000,000. If Company A has double the market capitalization of Company B in the same index fund, twice as much will be put into Company A's shares as Company B's.

Since index funds follow preset criteria and don't have to be actively managed, their expense ratios are much lower than traditional mutual funds. An index fund with an expense ratio of 0.25% would only cost you

$2.50 in fees for every $1,000 you have invested.

Index funds are great options because they're low-cost, hands-off, and almost always outperform actively-managed funds in the long run.

Exchange-traded funds (ETFs)

Like index funds, ETFs are designed to track different indexes. The difference is that ETFs are traded on the stock exchange and their prices fluctuate throughout the day like stocks. You can go to your broker and buy an ETF for whatever price it is at that moment – not the price of the fund at closing.

When you invest through your retirement account – like a 401(k) – you will usually do so through different funds, so it's important to grasp the general concept of how they work.

WHAT TO LOOK FOR

A common (and usually the first) mistake new investors make is thinking a stock's price represents its value. It's easy to mistakenly assume a $5 stock is cheap, and a $1,000 stock is expensive. A lot of people lose a lot of money making that assumption. It could very well be the case that the $5 stock is overpriced and the $1,000 stock is underpriced. A stock's price by itself is irrelevant. It's like deciding if you'd marry someone by only looking at their picture.

> *Refresher: EPS is a company's profit divided by the number of shares.*

Let's say we have two companies: Company A's shares are $20, and Company B's shares are $150. If you had $1,000 and I asked you if you'd rather buy 50 shares of Company A or 6 shares of Company B, you may be tempted to go with the 50 shares because more is better, right? Not quite. That's not how it always works with stocks.

Imagine Company A has an EPS of $2, and Company B has an EPS of $25. Would you still think taking the 50 shares of Company A was a better investment? (hint: the answer should be no). You couldn't decide this by only looking at the EPS, though.

You can figure this out by looking at the **price-earnings ratio** ("P/E ratio") — which is the price of a company's stock compared to how much they earn. You can find the P/E ratio by dividing a company's share price by its EPS. In this example, the ratios would be:

Company A's P/E ratio = ($20 share price) / ($2 EPS) = $10
Company B's P/E ratio = ($150 share price) / ($25 EPS) = $6

This means you're paying $10 for every $1 in earnings from Company A and $6 for every $1 in earnings from Company B. The smaller this number, the better. All other things equal, it wouldn't make sense *not* to go with Company B.

The P/E ratio gives you a much better idea of a stock's value than just looking at its price. To determine if a stock is overvalued, undervalued, or priced just right, compare its P/E ratio to the P/E ratio of other companies in its industry. You wouldn't want to compare ExxonMobil to Twitter, or Citi Trends to Berkshire Hathaway.

If you'd rather use 1-ply toilet paper than look through a company's financial statements and calculate their EPS, just do an internet search and get the amount. The goal is to work smarter, not harder.

Along with the P/E ratio, here are some things you need to consider before investing in a company:

• Do you want to invest in dividend stocks or growth stocks?

As we discussed earlier, when determining if an investment has been worthwhile, you need to look at the total return and not just the change in the stock's price. Since dividends make up the bulk of a stock's total return, you want to take that into consideration before choosing to invest into a company.

Dividend Stocks

Dividend stocks (which is an unofficial name given to stocks that pay high dividends) are great for long-term, passive income. Every three months you can count on receiving a payment — regardless of the company's share price.

You don't want to just look at the amount the company is paying out; you want to look at the payout amount relative to their stock's price. This is known as the **dividend yield**.

Dividend yield = annual dividend amount per share / the company's share price.

If a company with a $20 share price pays out $1 dividends quarterly, the dividend yield would be:

$4 / $20 = 0.25 or **25%**

You use $4 in the calculation because the $1 dividend is paid quarterly, not annually.

Don't fall for the dividend trap, though. Just because a company pays out a high dividend doesn't mean it's a good investment. In fact, a company paying out too high of a dividend is a red flag. Don't ignore red flags. The last time I ignored a red flag, I woke up with a shattered back window and a cinder block in my backseat. Don't ask me what the red flag was; just know that you should never ignore red flags.

You have to ask yourself *why* they're paying out so much instead of re-investing it in the company to try and grow.

Blue-chip stocks — which are well-known, well-established companies like Coca-Cola and Disney — are safe choices and are known to pay higher dividends to make up for the fact that their stocks don't move much in price.

Be skeptic of non-Blue-chip stocks that pay out excessively high dividend yields.

Growth stocks

On the other end of the spectrum, you have growth stocks. These stocks are sexier to the average person than dividend stocks. If dividend stocks are Amy Schumer, growth stocks are Rihanna.

Growth stocks are shares in companies that are expected to grow at a fast rate. These are typically newer, disruptive companies that are growing much faster than other companies in their industry.

Since these companies focus on growth, they typically don't pay dividends and instead re-invest the money back into the company. People who invest in growth stocks make their money from the capital gains when they eventually sell their shares. You have to be comfortable with not receiving consistent income for the chance at a huge cash-out in the future.

It's not a guarantee that a company will do well and its stock's price will rise. As a result, growth stocks are risky because that's the only way investor's make money from them.

Do what's comfortable for you, but as with anything investment related, diversification is important. Many investors try to include both dividend and growth stocks in their portfolio.

Just like it's fair to assume that any middle-aged White man driving a Dodge Charger is the police, it's fair to assume that the prices of any stocks you own will be unpredictable. Choosing companies that pay out dividends along with growth stocks ensures you'll at least receive *some* return on your investments; even as the stock prices fluctuate.

- Do you know the business?

Don't invest in what you don't know. It may seem basic, but this is important. You are buying ownership in the company — why wouldn't you want to be knowledgeable about what they do?

You don't need to know every little detail of the company, but you should, at the bare minimum, know two things: how they make money and what's their competitive advantage.

The first one is simple. Do they sell products like Walmart and Target? Do they charge a subscription like Netflix and Spotify? Do they sell advertisements like Facebook and Google? Whatever the case may be, you should know it.

The second one may seem more complicated, but it's relatively simple as well. Is the company's strategy to sell products cheaper than everybody else like Dollar Tree? Do they sell high-end products at premium prices like Apple or BMW? Do they have strong brand recognition like Coca-Cola or McDonald's? Whatever the case may be, you should know it.

- How much money does the company make?

It's one thing to know how a company makes money, but you also want to know how much they make. You can find this on a company's **income statement** — which shows their revenue and profits for a given period.

A company's revenue is sometimes referred to as its "top line" because it's always the top line on a company's balance sheet. Their profit is referred to as the "bottom line" because it's always the bottom line on the balance sheet. Reading a balance sheet is like deciphering hieroglyphics for some people. Don't let all the other numbers confuse you; those are the two that really matter. In a basketball game it may be cool to look at all the team and player statistics, but ultimately, the only numbers that matter are the teams' final scores. The same applies here. Focus on what's important: How much they're making and how much is profit.

With smartphones at your fingertips, you can find this information with a simple internet search. Work smarter, not harder.

It's in your best interest to look into companies that have shown steady growth year-to-year, because it shows consistency and lets you know the company is continuing to grow and not being complacent. Companies are like relationships: once they get complacent and stagnant, they're headed towards failure. That's how the game goes.

As I stressed in the introduction of the book, I'm no investing guru, and honestly, you should be wary of anybody who says they are. Self-proclaimed investing "gurus" are to be as trusted as those 10 for $1.49 chicken nuggets from Burger King. I'm all for a bargain, but there's something about paying less than 15 cents for a chicken nugget that doesn't sit well with me. You can hardly buy a dime for 15 cents in this economy.

There's no foolproof investing plan or strategy. If it were, I'd be on a yacht in Croatia lighting Cuban cigars with $100 bills and sippin' Ace of Spades, instead of perfecting my "try samples in the food court at the mall and pretend like I'm actually interested in buying something" act. I can, however, assure you that if you take those things into consideration before choosing your investments, you'll be in a much better position.

You should always consult a professional financial advisor if you want specific investing recommendations.

WHY TO INVEST IN STOCKS

No need for an elaborate, drawn-out explanation on why you should invest in stocks. It really just boils down to their return potential compared to other securities, like bonds.

You take on higher risks for a chance at higher rewards. That's how life works.

BONDS

Bonds are interesting. A lot of people have heard of bonds, but not many know exactly what they are, or how they work. While stocks get all the attention and news coverage, bonds tend to get treated like Megan Griffin from Family Guy. If stocks are Michael Jackson, bonds are Tito Jackson.

When institutions — whether corporations or governments — need money, one of the ways that they get it is by issuing bonds. A government may issue bonds to pay for things like road improvement (apparently everywhere except Baltimore) and building schools, while a corporation may issue bonds to get money to conduct research or invest in the latest technology.

Unlike stocks, when you buy bonds, you're not purchasing ownership. Instead, you're loaning the issuer money so you can receive interest on it. That's why they're considered a debt security — whoever issued the bond owes the bondholders. It's the finance world's version of "Let me hold something, you know I'm good for it."

Although it's a loan, the repayments don't work like regular loans. Here's how bonds work:

The price a bond is initially sold for is its **face value** (or "par value"). The date it's initially sold is its **issue date**, and the end of its term is its **maturity date**.

Between the issue date and the maturity date, the issuer makes interest payments — called **coupon payments** — to the bondholder. Once the maturity date hits, the bondholder will receive back the face value of the bond.

Imagine that you buy a $1,000 bond on January 1, 2020 and it takes 10-years to mature. During those 10 years, you will receive coupon payments every six months and then on January 1, 2030 (the maturity date), you'll receive your original $1,000 back.

Even though coupon payments are made every six months, a bond's interest rate (or "coupon rate") is expressed annually. For example, if the $1,000 bond you bought had a 7% coupon rate you wouldn't receive a $70 payment twice a year, it would be two $35 payments.

Bonds that don't pay coupon payments are called **zero-coupon bonds**. They're sold below face value, so instead of making money from coupon payments, you make money from the difference in price of what you bought it for and its face value. You may purchase a bond with a $5,000 face value for $4,500 and then pocket the $500 difference on its maturity date.

Those are the two primary ways to make money from bonds: the coupon payments, and buying it below face value and holding it until it matures.

Just like consumers can default on their debts, an institution can default on a bond if it's unable to pay coupon payments to its bondholders. If that happens, then you will be unable to collect your full amount on the maturity date.

TYPES OF BONDS

There are three primary types of bonds: Treasury, municipal, and corporate.

Treasury bonds

Treasury bonds are issued by the U.S. government and are backed by the "full faith and credit" of the government, meaning they're considered risk-free. Granted, no investment is 100% risk-free, but Treasury bonds are as close as it gets. Think of them being 99.99% risk-free. It's like betting on the ice cream machine being broken at your local McDonald's. Can you imagine Uncle Sam hitting you with an "I ain't got it right now, fam" when it's time to receive your coupon payment or get the face value back?

This lack of risk means the returns on these bonds are very low. A risk-free investment with high returns would be too good to be true, right? That's like a Hummer with good gas mileage.

Treasury securities are given different names based on when they mature:

- Treasury bills mature in one year or less, and are zero-coupon bonds.
- Treasury notes can mature in 2, 3, 5, 7, or 10 years.

- Treasury bonds usually mature in 30 years.

Don't let the differences in names confuse you, they're all technically bonds.

One good thing about Treasury bonds is that they can be bought directly from the U.S. Treasury by just going to their website and making an account. You can still get them through your broker but going directly through the U.S. Treasury avoids commission fees. The problem with this, however, is that the government doesn't sell them very often — only four times per year. So, unless you buy them during those times, you'll have to cop them off the secondary market.

Municipal bonds

Municipal bonds ("Munis") are issued by state and local governments. These bonds are usually issued to fund projects like infrastructure improvement, building hospitals and community centers, and other projects that benefit the residents of that government.

There are two types of municipal bonds: general obligation and revenue. Both of them serve the same purpose. The only difference is how the issuer gets the money to pay you back.

General obligation bonds are backed by that government's taxing power. In other words, your payments come from tax revenue. If times get rough and they need money to pay bondholders, they could always just increase certain taxes. Don't you wish you had that power?

Revenue bonds are paid out from the money generated by the project the bond was used to fund. For example, if a city issues municipal bonds to upgrade a toll system, the money paid to bondholders would come from the revenue earned by the tolls.

The interest earned from municipal bonds is exempt from federal taxes, and it may also be exempt from state and local taxes if you live where the bonds were issued. This is called "double exempt." Because of the major tax benefits, the coupon rate offered on these tends to be on the lower end.

A default on a municipal bond is like finding a White person who has never been to a Dave Matthews concert before – it's rare, but it can happen.

Corporate bonds

Take a stab in the dark and guess who issues corporate bonds. If you guessed corporations, you're correct. If you guessed anything else, seek help.

Corporate bonds are typically sold in $1,000 increments, and the coupon rates and maturity times vary widely.

They're backed solely by the ability of the company to make payments, which makes them riskier than Treasury and municipal bonds. Because there are thousands of companies that issue bonds and not all of them have the same ability to pay their bondholders (as I'm sure you can imagine), there is a rating system to let investors know how risky a bond is.

RATINGS

Just like people have credit scores that let lenders know how likely they are to pay back a loan, bonds have a rating that let investors know their riskiness. These ratings are used to indicate a bond issuers ability to pay back the face value and make coupon payments on time.

Three companies are responsible for rating bonds: Standard and Poor, Fitch, and Moody's. They do a lot of the hard work for you. Ratings range from "AAA" to "D," with AAA being the least risky. A bond with a "D" rating is about as safe as a Steve-O stunt.

This is how the three companies rate bonds:

BOND RATINGS CHART			
MOODY'S	S&P	FITCH	
Aaa	AAA	AAA	
Aa1	AA+	AA+	
Aa2	AA	AA	
Aa3	AA-	AA-	
A1	A+	A+	INVESTMENT GRADE
A2	A	A	
A3	A-	A-	
Baa1	BBB+	BBB+	
Baa2	BBB	BBB	
Baa3	BBB-	BBB-	
Ba1	BB+	BB+	
Ba2	BB	BB	
Ba3	BB-	BB-	
B1	B+	B+	
B2	B	B	
B3	B-	B-	
Caa1	CCC+	CCC+	JUNK
Caa2	CCC	CCC	
Caa3	CCC-	CCC-	
Ca	CC	CC+	
	C	CC	
		CC-	
D	D	DDD	

As the chart shows, depending on its rating, a bond with either be considered investment-grade or a junk-bond. And while the exact science behind the ratings isn't really significant, we know rating agencies look at

a company's income, expenses, assets, debts, and financial history to give them a score. Once a company hits the junk grade, you know their finances are beginning to look funny in the light.

As a result of their riskiness, junk bonds tend to offer higher coupon rates to give people an incentive to buy the bonds. After all, why would you buy a junk bond if you could get the same return with a less-risky investment-grade bond?

As with any investment, you should at least do some research on your own. Don't put all of your faith into a bond's rating.

WHY PEOPLE BUY BONDS

There are five main reasons why people invest in bonds.

1) Most of them are safe.

One of the things that stop a lot of people from investing is the risk involved. The only exact science to guarantee that you don't lose money when investing is to not invest. Some people literally can't afford to take the chances.

Bonds offer a much safer alternative to stocks. Not only is a default unlikely with investment-grade bonds, but if things take a turn for the worse and a company must go bankrupt, bondholders get priority over shareholders when it comes to being paid. It makes sense that they'd pay the people they borrowed money from before paying the people who willingly took ownership in the company (and consequently took on the risks associated with it).

As the bond rating system shows, not all bonds are safe investments. However, with options like Treasury and municipal bonds, there are incredibly safe options out there that even the most financially-conservative person can stomach.

2) A reliable source of income.

Of course, you'd hope that all of your investments are reliable sources of income, but this isn't always the reality. Companies and economies go through rough times. That's life. Luckily for bondholders, these rough times seldom affect their coupon payments. Every six months, you can count on your money coming in. Coupon payments are more stable than dividend payments, because companies are legally obligated to pay the interest on their bonds before they can even think about paying out stock dividends. After all, *they* borrowed money from *you*. That would be like watching your homie flexin' and buying bottles in the club while they owe you money.

3) They can be better than savings accounts.

Interest rates on savings accounts at a lot of banks (especially larger ones) are terrible, fam. In certain accounts, your money is basically sitting around collecting mold, instead of making money for you. There's nothing necessarily wrong with this though because regardless of how small, you're earning *something* and not losing money. Some bonds give a comparably safe alternative, with higher returns. If you're not going to need the money soon (ideally within a year), you could be getting more bang for your buck.

Note: I'm not suggesting you replace your savings account. You still need one. But, if you have an emergency fund (three to six months' worth of living expenses) in a savings account, that additional money can be better served where the returns are better.

If you're saving for a life event like your child's college tuition or retirement, this is also a useful saving strategy because you know exactly how much you're going to earn from the bond in a given time frame. You can plan your saving contributions accordingly.

4) They diversify your investment portfolio.

Everyone has heard the phrase "don't put all your eggs in one basket." This is especially true when it comes to investing. Given the instability of stocks, having bonds in your investment portfolio can help preserve some of your money when the stock market is plummeting. Bonds ensure that you will at least have *some* money coming in from the coupon payments, and you can count on your principal being there.

The exact percentage of your investments that should be in bonds is based on your financial situation, of course. However, a good rule of thumb is to subtract your age from 110, and that's the percentage of stocks that you should have. The rest should be in bonds or a different class of investments.

For example, if you're 25 years old, you should aim to have your investment portfolio consist of roughly 85% stocks and 15% bonds/other. The idea is that as you get older, you should become more conservative with your investments because you'll have less time to bounce back if things turn sour.

5) The Tax advantages are great.

Unless held in a non-taxable retirement account like a 401(k), your earnings from stocks are taxable. Bonds offer more lucrative tax advantages than stocks.

U.S. Treasury bonds are exempt from state and local taxes, and municipal bonds are exempt from federal taxes (and potentially state/local taxes as well).

THE POWER OF "NOW" AND COMPOUND INTEREST

Regardless of whether you're investing in stocks or investing in bonds, the real power of investing comes from **compound interest**. In investing, compound interest is your best friend and truly shows how you can put your money to work for you. Earning money from investments – whether from dividends or coupon payments – is undoubtedly a good thing; nobody is arguing against that. The real benefit of investing, however, comes from re-investing these earnings and letting the interest earn interest on itself.

Let's take a look at a very simple example: if you have $1,000 and earn 10% in interest, you'll have $1,100. If you earn 10% on that amount, then you'll have $1,210. If you then earn 10% on that amount, you'll have $1,331. The cycle continues.

With compound interest, you made $331 in three flips. Had you removed the profit after each payment and just left the original $1,000, you would've only made $300. That $31 difference shows the power of compound interest. This is a small-scale example, of course, but nonetheless it shows the benefits of letting your interest earn interest.

Assuming that you're investing for the future (as you probably should be), it doesn't make sense not to re-invest profits and let that money make money. Instead of withdrawing your dividend or coupon payments and spending that money, treat it like you do "terms and conditions" and ignore it. You'll start to really see the power of compound interest.

More than anything, time is the most crucial factor when it comes to benefitting from compound interest. There's a saying that goes, "the best time to invest was yesterday. The next best time is today." The sooner that you begin investing, no matter the amount, the sooner you can begin having your money make money for you.

To show the power of compound interest, let's say that we have three people ages 25, 35, and 45. They each invest an initial $100 and set aside $100 each month in an investment that earns 8% annually. By the age of 65, each of them would've accumulated the following amounts:

25-year-old: $351,528
35-year-old: $150,129
45-year-old: $59,394

The 25-year-old only contributed $12,000 more than the 35-year-old during that time, yet earned more than $200,000 more. The differences in numbers speak for themselves. Time really is money!

If you're not getting into investing with the intentions of taking advantage of compound interest, you're missing a huge point of investing. In fact, some people might argue that you're missing *the* point.

CRYPTOCURRENCY

Let's just be honest here: you're confused. Your homies 'nem are confused. Your parents are confused, and we damn sure know that your grandparents — who probably still use a phone with T9 texting abilities — are confused. Hell, everybody's confused.

Watch the news or get on the internet for longer than 30 minutes and at some point, you're bound to hear the words Bitcoin or cryptocurrency. Even if you try to avoid it, they seem to pop up when you least expect it. Kinda like those monthly Apple Music payments.

At a fundamental level, cryptocurrency is just digital money. The prefix "crypto" makes it sound complex, but the idea of it is relatively simple.

Bitcoin, the name that you're probably used to hearing, is a type of cryptocurrency, but it's not the only type. It just so happens to be the first, and most important. I'll try to explain cryptocurrency as a whole, and then focus in on Bitcoin and how it works.

I won't be giving advice on how to invest in cryptocurrency, but hopefully after reading this, you'll at least know how cryptocurrency works and how to get started if you decide to invest in it.

WHY IT MATTERS

Cryptocurrency is relatively new, but the idea of digital cash is not. Folks had been attempting to create a digital cash that was worth a damn since the '90s, but they were about as successful as Stevie Wonder would be in an archery competition.

When Bitcoin was initially released in 2009, the most appealing attribute that separated it from previous digital cash attempts was that it was de-centralized. That's what makes cryptocurrency, cryptocurrency.

Countries have central banks in place (the U.S. has the Federal Reserve, for example) that are in charge of enforcing policies, controlling the money supply, determining interest rates, etc. Cryptocurrencies being decentralized means that there's no need for these institutions — it's 100% peer-to-peer, compadre-to-compadre, business-to-business. No middlemen involved.

Cryptocurrency takes the borders away from earth. It can be sent virtually anywhere without having to go through third-party companies like Visa, PayPal, or Western Union, that charge fees for transactions.

More importantly, it takes big banks and traditional financial institutions out the picture, like a deadbeat dad.

If you're not familiar with the 2008 financial crisis, let me sum it up in a couple of sentences: A bunch of old White men in fancy suits at banks and financial institutions gambled with consumer's money and lost...BIG. I'm talking skunked in the first quarter type of loss. This forced the government to spend $700 billion of taxpayers' money to bail them out. That's a lot of money, dawg. Since then, the trust towards financial institutions has been running thinner than European supermodels.

Learning how cryptocurrency works will help you understand how that problem is solved.

How it works

Explaining how Bitcoin works can get a little confusing without using real-life analogies that help paint the picture, so I'll try to do just that.

Bitcoin operates on what is called **blockchain** technology. This blockchain technology collects and stores all Bitcoin transactions that have ever been made. Every 10 minutes, any transaction that has been performed during that time slot is collected into a block, and then added to previous blocks; creating a long chain of blocks. Hence the name blockchain. Every transaction that has ever been made is permanently recorded on the public blockchain. The people who collect these transactions and verify that they're legit are called **Miners**.

This entire process works like your favorite nightclub. Not the type of club that won't let you in because you're wearing Jordans, but will let Spencer with the rundown Sperrys and wrinkled khakis in either. Imagine Liv on Sunday or Magic City Monday.

People in line outside = Transactions
Bouncer = Miners
Club = Blockchain

Imagine the bouncer advancing the line every 10 minutes (you know clubs like to hold lines). He checks their IDs, charges a cover, and then allows them into the club. For imaginary purposes, let's assume that the bouncer records the amount paid by each individual and time stamps each transaction with a unique identifier. That's how the blockchain works.

There are tons of miners around the world working independently that are keeping the network powered. This is what keeps Bitcoin decentralized. The network doesn't rely on one institution or person to keep it running. If the government shuts down Bitcoin in one country, the network keeps running smoothly because there are always miners working in other parts of the world.

How to buy

With so much chaos going on in the cryptocurrency world, it's easy for beginners to become overwhelmed.

As with stocks, you buy cryptocurrencies on exchanges. Cryptocurrency exchanges allow you to buy and sell cryptocurrencies using cash. You open an account with the exchange, transfer money into that account from your bank account, and then purchase cryptocurrencies on the exchange. It works much like traditional brokerage companies.

If you're new to cryptocurrency investing, it's probably in your best interest to stick with apps like Coinbase or Robinhood that have become reliable staples in the cryptocurrency world. They're extremely user-friendly and relatively easy to start.

After you create your account, you have the option to fund it either via bank or debit/credit card. Using a bank has a cheaper fee, but it takes 3-5 business days for the money to hit your exchange account. Using a card funds the account almost immediately, but has a much higher fee. Ultimately, it's a matter of convenience and fees.

You can buy a portion of a cryptocurrency. You don't have to buy the whole thing. It's like a Sbarro pizza. For example, if the price of Bitcoin is at $10,000 (which is ironically about the cost of a whole Sbarro pizza) and you only have $2,000, you can buy 0.2 Bitcoin (BTC). Hell, if you only have $10, you can buy 0.001 Bitcoin. Just like $1 can be broken down into quarters, dimes, nickels, and pennies, one Bitcoin can be broken down into 100,000,000 units — called satoshis, which is named after the anonymous founder.

Storing cryptocurrency

Similar to regular cash, Bitcoin and other cryptocurrencies need to be stored. Just as cash can be stored in different ways — such as a wallet, bank, or under the mattress – cryptocurrencies can be stored in various ways. There are software and hardware wallets.

Luckily, a lot of exchanges will also function as a wallet; so you don't have to worry about buying on one platform and storing on another. Hardware wallets, on the other hand, are physical storage devices that are essentially USB drives. Software wallets are better if you plan to trade relatively often, and hardware wallets are for long-term holding.

When you get a wallet, you'll have a public key which you will use to send and receive cryptocurrencies, and a private key which gives you actual access to your cryptocurrencies (almost like an online banking PIN).

With software wallets, you leave your private key in the hands of the company and trust that they'll keep them secured. The majority of them do, but it's not 100% guaranteed with all platforms. There's a chance the platform could crash, and considering cryptocurrencies are unregulated, there's nothing legally stopping these platforms from just closing their site and disappearing into thin air with your money like David Blaine.

With hardware wallets, it's on you to guard your private key like Deion Sanders in his prime. Just like somebody can take your wallet with all of your money in it, they can take your hardware wallet with your cryptocurrencies stored on it.

Investing-ish

I'ma keep it real with you. When it comes to investing in cryptocurrencies, it's like the Wild West, fam. Investing in general carries risks, but investing in cryptocurrencies is "reaching for your wallet in front of the police as a Black man" type risky. A lot of traditional investors are even hesitant to consider it investing, but more so speculating.

One of the main issues with investing in cryptocurrencies is it's nearly impossible to figure out the worth. With actual businesses, plenty of different metrics (like revenue, profits, and such) can be used to determine their value. Since cryptocurrencies don't generate cash, it doesn't quite work that way.

Nobody really knows the true long-term outlook of cryptocurrencies. Some folks believe it will be the new universal currency of the world, and others think that it will come and go quicker than a henna tattoo.

Regardless of which side you agree with, there's one piece of advice I give anybody looking to invest in cryptocurrencies: don't put more money in cryptocurrencies than you'd be willing to lose gambling in Vegas — because that's essentially what you're doing.

CHAPTER FOUR

RETIREMENT

"Gucci can't retire 'cause he ain't made a hundred mill yet."
—GUCCI MANE

Note: This chapter will be more beneficial if you've read the section on funds in the Investing chapter.

Some people dream of the day that they can retire, move to a tropical location, and sit around drinking cocktails on the beach all day. Some dream of retiring and finally being able to focus on a hobby that they love doing full-time. And some, quite frankly, dream of retiring and doing absolutely nothing — they just want to wake up in the comforts of their own home with no responsibilities except to eat, shit, and shower.

Whatever you dream of doing in retirement, one thing's for sure: you're going to need money. That's about as certain as Black folks keeping plastic bags underneath their kitchen sinks.

Being able to retire is a beautiful thing. Being able to retire and still live comfortably during those years is even more beautiful. If you're working during your retirement years, it should be because you want to, not out of necessity. Unfortunately, most minorities aren't in that position. Reports show that the typical Black household only has around $19,000 in retirement savings, while a White household has over $130,000. Of course, income equality has a lot to do with this; it's hard to save money that you don't have. But, lack of access to (and knowledge of) retirement accounts also plays a significant role in the disparity. Minorities are more likely to work a lower-wage or part-time job, so many don't have access to employer-sponsored retirement plans like a 401(k), and even fewer have an IRA. This means saving and planning for retirement falls solely on them. This lower access to retirement accounts directly correlates to households having less in retirement savings.

Even those with the access tend to not take full advantage of it. They either don't use the plans at all, or they don't understand the investment options enough to be able to make informed decisions.

We'll cover two of the most popular retirement accounts — 401(k)'s and IRAs.

401(K)

A 401(k) is an employer-based retirement savings plan. It allows you to save and invest a portion of your paycheck, before taxes are taken out. Having this money deducted from your paycheck pre-tax is clutch because it lowers your taxable income. If your paycheck is $1,000, but you decide to contribute 10% to your 401(k), only $900 of your paycheck will be taxed.

If you work for a nonprofit, school district, religious organization, or government organization, this retirement plan is called a 403(b). It functions the same way as a 401(k) account; the only notable difference is the name. Throughout the chapter, I'll be using "401(k)" but know that the information applies to both.

Unlike a regular savings account where your money is sitting around collecting dust like black furniture, the money in your 401(k) is invested. You don't get to pick out individual stocks, however. Your employer will usually present you with different funds for you to choose from.

It's on you to decide how you want to allocate your contributions. It may seem overwhelming and complicated at first, but it doesn't have to be. You don't need an MBA to make good 401(k) investment decisions. And you damn sure don't need one to make better 401(k) investment decisions than I did. The first time I ever went to select my 401(k) investments, I was as lost as Ray Charles in a corn maze. I didn't know what the hell I was looking at. Just a few weeks earlier I was pouring water in an empty liquid soap bottle to try and stretch it out. At that point, I was just happy to have a job; the last thing on my mind was a 401(k).

When in doubt, these methods are reliable go-to options: target date funds and model portfolios. They aren't necessarily foolproof, but they're like buying someone a gift card for Christmas — you can never go wrong with it.

Target Date Funds

Target date funds make investing for retirement as simple as walking and chewing gum at the same time (kinda). If investing is a foreign language to you, and you want a quick and simple "set it and go on about your business" type of option, these funds may be best for you. You'll know it's a target date fund because it will have a year in its name — like "StackYoBread 2040 Fund."

You will want to decide your approximate retirement year, and then choose the fund closest to that date. Let's say you're 25 and plan to retire at 65. You would want to pick a target date fund that has a date that is close to 40 years from now. If it's 2020, select the "StackYoBread 2060 Fund."

The fund automatically re-balances for you as time goes on. The further you are from retirement, the more aggressive the portfolio will be (meaning it will be mostly composed of stocks). As you get older, it will get more conservative, and you can expect to see fewer stocks and more bonds. If you haven't noticed by now, that's a common theme in investing.

Once you pick an estimate retirement date and choose the appropriate fund for you, that's it. Put your contributions there, and you're done.

Crossing the street in Times Square is harder than that.

Model portfolio

If your 401(k) plan doesn't offer any target date funds — or if you prefer to be more hands-on with your investments — you can go with a model portfolio.

Model portfolios allow you to pick a portfolio based on your risk tolerance. The portfolios range from "conservative" to "aggressive," with several balanced options in between.

A conservative portfolio will avoid risks and be mostly investment-grade bonds that you don't have to worry about. Your money might grow slower than the last hour of work, but it'll be growing, nonetheless.

An aggressive portfolio is out to hit a grand slam and find the next Amazon. Of course, the risks are much greater and you could lose money, but there's a possibility for huge gains. For a lot of younger people, the risk is worth taking. Worst-case scenario, you lose money that you have decades to make back. Best-case scenario, you make a lot of damn money.

As a general rule of thumb, the further you are from retirement, the more risk you can handle. Of course, everybody isn't comfortable taking the same risks, so always do what's comfortable for you — and only what's comfortable for you.

You don't have to put all of your money into one option. You can divide it up however you see fit. You could put 100% in a target date fund, or you could put 60% in a target fund and 40% in an aggressive portfolio. It's completely up to you.

Either way, once you set it, the hard part is over. You may want to rebalance your 401(k) every now and then, just to make sure that it's still aligned with your goals and risk tolerance, but that shouldn't be something that you do regularly.

Contributing

Now that you have a general idea of where you want your money to go, it's time to figure out just how much to put into your 401(k). When it comes to contributing to your 401(k), you get to decide a percentage of your paycheck that you want deducted. The IRS limits yearly contributions to $19,000 ($24,500 if you're 50 or older), so keep this in mind when deciding how much to contribute.

One thing that I often stress is that you need to be sure to have an emergency fund set aside in a regular savings account before maxing out your contributions.

A sufficient emergency fund will have at least six months of living expenses in it. If you're younger with no kids, you can get away with three months, but six is recommended. Imagine if you lost your job today. Would you be able to survive six months with your current bills if you didn't earn a single penny during that time? If the answer is "no" (which it is for a lot of people), focus on getting it to a "yes" before you start getting trigger happy with the 401(k) contributions.

If life ever comes at you fast and you need access to emergency funds, it'll be 10x easier — and much, much cheaper — to get it from a savings account than it would be if you had to withdraw it from your 401(k).

If you're younger than 59 ½ years old and choose to withdraw from your 401(k), not only will you have to pay income taxes on the amount, you will also have to pay a 10% penalty tax. Depending on the amount, you could end up with as little as half of what you withdrew. Oftentimes, it's just not worth it, which is why the emergency fund is more important initially.

For example, let's assume that you don't have an emergency fund and a crisis pops up that requires $20,000. If you withdraw $20,000 from your 401(k) and are in the 22% tax bracket, it will cost you $6,400:

$20,000 * 10% fee = $2,000
$20,000 * 22% income tax = $4,400

When it's all said and done, you will only receive $13,600. That's Uncle Sam robbing you in broad daylight with no mask on.

That's why it's so important to have an emergency fund. If that $20,000 was in a savings account, you could withdraw it for $free.99.

Companies will often match your contributions up to a certain percentage. If you're a 4/20-friendly person, you're likely familiar with the term "matching." Well, it works just like that. You should at least contribute the highest percentage that your company is willing to match. If you don't, you're giving away free money. That's hustlin' backwards.

That percentage should also be the most that you contribute until you have your emergency fund at a level that you're comfortable with. If your company matches up to 5%, only contribute 5%. Nothing more, nothing less.

If you're in debt, you should focus on paying down your debt versus upping your 401(k) contribution. Debt comes with interest so the longer it sits around, the more expensive it becomes. Be sure to make it a priority. If you're still relatively young, there's no sense in trying to save a ton for retirement at the expense of staying in debt. That's about as smart as eating a Popeye's biscuit without a drink.

Borrowing

Sometimes the amount in your emergency fund just isn't enough, and you may have to resort to your 401(k). That's nothing to be embarrassed about it. It happens every day, B. If this is the case, you can either choose to withdraw money directly from your 401(k) and take the taxes and penalty on the chin, or you can choose to borrow money from your 401(k).

Borrowing money from your 401(k) can seem like a weird concept considering that it's your money, but it works like a loan. You even pay yourself back the money with interest. If you're employed, the repayments will be taken directly out your paychecks after-taxes and put back into your 401(k). If you can't repay the loan, it will be treated as a withdrawal and the taxes and 10% fee will be applied. Luckily, a 401(k) loan default won't show up on your credit report. Can you imagine your credit score taking a hit because you couldn't pay back a loan you borrowed from yourself? That'd be humbling.

The maximum that you can borrow is either $50,000 or 50% of what you contributed; whichever is less. You will usually have up to five years to repay the loan unless you took it out to buy a house, and in that case, you may have longer terms.

Fees

It may be true that the best things in life are free. Your 401(k), however, is not. An alarming amount of people with 401(k)s have no idea how much they're paying in fees. Even worse, many people don't even know that they're paying fees at all. That's…not good.

All DMVs have a long wait, all apartment complexes that end with "Heights" or "Terrace" are in the hood, and all 401(k) plans have fees. That's life. 401(k) fees fall into one of three categories: investment, administration, or service.

- Investment

Investment fees include the cost of managing your investments, and other investment-related services. They're charged as a percentage of your investment assets and will usually be the most expensive of your fees.

- Administration

Your 401(k) doesn't manage itself. Whoever manages your plan – whether it's a bank or other financial institution – isn't doing so out of the kindness of their heart. Administration fees cover things like accounting, record-keeping, and legal services.

- Service

These fees are charged for additional services or features you may decide to opt into and use – like taking out a 401(k) loan.

Rarely (if ever) would you purchase a subscription without knowing the price, right? The same should apply to your 401(k). Don't blindly opt into something without knowing how much it's going to cost you. Granted, I know it's easier to understand subscription costs when it's as straightforward as paying X amount of dollars each month; I get it. But, this is your financial well-being we're talking about – it's worth knowing how those fees work.

If your investments return 8% but you're paying 1.5% in fees, your real return is only 6.5%. On the surface, that 1.5% doesn't seem like much, but don't underestimate just how much money that equals in the long run. Let's assume you have 30 years left until retirement and your 401(k) balance is currently $30,000. If you never contribute another penny to your account and average 8% in annual returns, this how much your balance would be with each respective fee:

1%: $228,500
1.5%: $198,500

Note: numbers are rounded to the nearest $500

If I told you there's a 0.5% difference in fees, you probably wouldn't blink. If I told you that the same 0.5% represents $30,000 over 30 years, your eyes might get bigger than the Powderpuff Girls'. In this scenario, a 0.5% difference in fees reduces your total balance by 13% in retirement. The fees matter. They could be the difference between sippin' mai tai's on a beach in Hawaii, or sippin' Coors Lights at a Motel 6 in Kansas.

Larger companies with more employees will typically pay less in fees

than smaller companies. Regardless of your company's size, any 401(k) fee above 1% is highway robbery.

Changing Jobs

Since 401(k) plans are company-sponsored, the account doesn't automatically follow you like your shadow when you change jobs. After switching jobs, you'll have four options for your 401(k): roll the money over to your new employer's plan, keep the money in your old employer's plan, cash the money out, or move it to an Individual Retirement Account ("IRA").

- Rolling the money over to your new employer's 401(k) plan

More often than not, your new 401(k) plan will accept rollovers from old retirement accounts. This option is good because your retirement money is in one location, and you won't have to worry about checking multiple accounts to try and keep up with your 401(k) money. The downside is that your new plan may have worse investment options or higher fees than your old plan.

- Keeping the money in your old employer's 401(k) plan

If you have at least $5,000 in your 401(k), you may be able to leave your money with your old employer. If you have less than that, they will usually cash you out, or require you to move the money within 60 days. It's like $5,000 gets you a "Make yourself comfortable," and anything less gets you a "You ain't gotta go home, but you gotta get the hell up outta here."

Keeping money in an old plan is only worth it if the investment options that they offer are considerably better, or the fees are significantly cheaper than your new plan. Otherwise, I wouldn't recommend it. If you get in the habit of leaving plans behind at jobs, you'll have a collection of 401(k)s scattered everywhere like Mattress Firms by the time that you retire. That makes it extremely hard to manage your money.

- Cashing the money out

Rarely is this the best option. As with any early withdrawal from your 401(k), cashing out when switching jobs involves paying taxes and a 10% penalty fee.

- Moving your money to an Individual Retirement Account (IRA)

Your last option is to transfer the money from your old 401(k) plan to an IRA. One advantage of an IRA is the large selection of investment options. Unlike a 401(k) where your employer picks the investments options that you can choose from, with an IRA you can choose any stock, bond, fund, or asset you choose. If 401(k) selections are the In-N-Out menu, IRA selections are the Cook Out menu.

You can rollover your money one of two ways: directly or indirectly. A direct rollover is when the money is transferred directly between the accounts. An indirect rollover involves your old plan sending you a check, and then you being responsible for depositing it into your new account. Personally, I don't see a valid reason why you'd want to do an indirect rollover if a direct rollover is an option, but humans have never been known for being rational.

If you go the indirect route, you will have 60 days to deposit the check into another account to avoid paying taxes and the 10% fee. You can only do this once every 12 years.

IRA

An Individual Retirement Account ("IRA") is similar to a 401(k) in that it's an account used to invest money for retirement, but there are very distinct differences between them. To begin, an IRA isn't tied to your employer. You must open your own IRA through a bank, brokerage company, or other financial institution. The contribution limit is also much lower for an IRA. The most you can contribute annually is $6,000 ($7,000 if you're 50 or older) — less than one-third of the 401(k) limit. (The contribution limit doesn't apply if you're rolling money over from another retirement account).

Choosing an IRA provider

Choosing an IRA provider ultimately comes down to your intentions. Do you plan to be an active investor, or do you plan to be hands-off?

If you plan to be more active and hands-on with your IRA, you should go with a traditional online broker. Here are five things to look for:

- Low (or no) account fees
- Low commission fees
- Commission-free ETFs
- Mutual funds with no transaction fees
- Accessible customer support

If you plan to be hands-off (which is the case for most people), a robo-advisor will work perfectly fine for you. They will automatically rebalance and reallocate your portfolio as time goes on. The main thing to look for in robo-advisors is the management fee. Never pay more than 0.5%.

Regardless of which provider you choose, the actual act of opening an account is no harder than opening a regular brokerage or bank account.

Types

There are two types of IRAs: Traditional and Roth. The difference between them comes down to one simple thing: when you have to pay taxes.

Traditional IRA

With a Traditional IRA, the contributions you make may be tax-deductible and won't be counted against your taxable income for the year. Instead, you will have to pay income tax on your contributions (and earnings) when you withdraw your money in retirement.

Although anyone can have a traditional IRA, not everyone is eligible for the full tax deduction. Your eligibility to deduct your contributions depends on your income and if you (or your spouse) is currently participating in a 401(k) plan. If you're not married, and not participating in a 401(k) plan, you can contribute up to the limit regardless of how much money you make. If you (or your spouse) are participating in a 401(k) plan, the amount you can deduct is income-based and may be limited.

These charts show the income range for deductions:

Traditional IRA deductions if you are participating in a 401(k) plan

FILING STATUS	INCOME	DEDUCTION
SINGLE	$64,000 or less	Full
SINGLE	$74,000 or more	Not eligible
MARRIED, FILING TOGETHER	$103,000 or less	Full
MARRIED, FILING TOGETHER	$123,000 or more	Not eligible
MARRIED, FILING SEPARATE	Less than $10,000	Full
MARRIED, FILING SEPARATE	$10,000 or more	Not eligible

*Traditional IRA deductions if you are **not** participating in a 401(k) plan*

FILING STATUS	INCOME	DEDUCTION
SINGLE	Any amount	Full
MARRIED AND YOUR SPOUSE DOESN'T HAVE AN ACTIVE 401(K) PLAN	Any amount	Full
MARRIED (FILING JOINTLY) AND YOUR SPOUSE HAS AN ACTIVE 401(K) PLAN	$193,000 or less	Full
	$203,000 or more	Not eligible
MARRIED (FILING SEPARATELY) AND YOUR SPOUSE HAS AN ACTIVE 401(K) PLAN	Less than $10,000	Full
	$10,000 or more	Not eligible

Anybody whose income falls between the 'full' and 'not eligible' limits is in the **phase-out range** and will only be eligible for a partial deduction.

Like a 401(k), if you withdraw from your Traditional IRA before you're 59½ years old, you will have to pay taxes, and you'll get smacked with a 10% penalty fee.

Also, with a traditional IRA, you're required to start taking mandatory taxable withdrawals from your account once you hit 70½ years old. Uncle Sam gave you a tax incentive up front with intentions of getting his money on the back-end; this is his way of saying, "it's been long enough, I need that tax money up off of you."

Here are some things to keep in mind with Traditional IRAs:

- There's no income limit when it comes to contributing to a Traditional IRA. The limit only applies to the tax deduction.
- You can no longer make contributions after age 70½. They cut you off like a bartender does when you start slurring your words and telling every stranger in sight that you love them.
- You can withdraw money early without being penalized for certain educational expenses (you will still owe taxes).
- You can withdraw up to $10,000 early without being penalized to buy your first crib (you will still owe taxes).

Roth IRA

Unlike a Traditional IRA, your Roth IRA contributions aren't tax-deductible. Instead, you contribute after-tax money, and then your contributions (and earnings) can be withdrawn tax-free in retirement. Roth IRA contribution limits are based on your income and filing status.

If you're single and make less than $122,000 annually, you can contribute the full limit. If you make $137,000 or more, you're not eligible to contribute to a Roth IRA. If you're in the phase-out range, you can contribute a partial amount.

This chart shows the income limits for Roth IRAs in 2019:

FILING STATUS	INCOME	CONTRIBUTION
SINGLE	Less than $122,000	Full
SINGLE	$137,000 or more	Not eligible
MARRIED, FILING JOINTLY	Less than $193,000	Full
MARRIED, FILING JOINTLY	$203,000 or more	Not eligible
MARRIED, FILING SEPARATELY	Less than $10,000	Full
MARRIED, FILING SEPARATELY	$10,000 or more	Not eligible

You can withdraw your contributions – but *not* earnings – from your Roth IRA at any time, without any penalties or taxes. After all, you've already paid taxes on the money you contributed; Uncle Sam can't get you again. You may, however, have to pay taxes and penalties on your earnings if you withdraw them early.

You want to make sure you plan on having your Roth IRA for at least five years when you open an account. After you've had your Roth IRA for at least five years, you may be able to withdraw your earnings penalty-free (you will still pay taxes).

Unlike a Traditional IRA, Roth IRAs don't require you to ever make withdrawals from your account. You can pass the account on to your children like a baton if you so choose to.

If you can live your life comfortably without touching the money in your Roth IRA, why not leave it there and let it continue to grow exponentially?

Passing a Roth IRA on to your children is a great way to try and establish generational wealth.

Here are some things to keep in mind with Roth IRAs:

- There is an income limit when it comes to being able to contribute to a Roth IRA. If you make enough money to not qualify for a Roth IRA, I don't feel bad for you. Chalk it up to the game.
- There are no mandatory withdrawals in retirement.

What's right for you?

Ultimately, deciding which account type is right for you can be broken down to the tax bracket you're in now compared to where you believe you'll be in retirement.

If you're a fairly recent graduate and haven't been in the workforce long, it may benefit you more to go with a Roth IRA because chances are you'll be in a higher tax bracket by the time that you retire. It makes sense to pay taxes now while you're in a lower bracket, instead of later when it will be costlier.

If you're in your peak earning years and this is likely to be the highest tax bracket you'll be in, it may make sense to go with a Traditional IRA so you won't have to pay taxes until you're in a lower tax bracket.

Take advantage of the tax benefits

IRAs, regardless of the type, are a gift from the IRS. Uncle Sam is usually stingy enough to make Julius from *Everybody Hates Chris* seem like a philanthropist, so whenever you can take advantage of a tax benefit, be sure to do just that.

Roth IRAs are even more of a gift.

Unlike brokerage accounts (which are taxable), IRAs allow your investments to grow tax-free. Any stock that grows in value will earn you more in a Roth IRA than it will in a brokerage account. If a stock goes from $10 to $30 in an IRA account, that $20 profit is all yours in retirement. If the same thing happens in a brokerage account, you'll owe taxes on the $20 when you sell the stock.

Like investing in general, the real power of Roth IRAs comes from re-invested dividends and compound interest. In a regular brokerage account, you pay taxes on the dividends you earn as you receive them. In a Roth IRA, the dividends you earn aren't taxed, which means the full amount can be re-invested.

Imagine that you invest in a company that pays out $100 in dividends one year. In an IRA, you can re-invest that full $100. In a brokerage account, that $100 would be taxed. If the tax rate is 10%, you will only have $90 to re-invest. This $10 difference may seem small, but when you look at the compounding effect, you'll see just how much it's *really* worth.

Let's assume you invested an initial $5,000 in a company that grew 8% each year, and paid out 2% in dividends.

Here's how your earnings would stack up after 20 years in a Roth IRA:

YEAR	THIS YEAR'S RETURN	TOTAL RETURNS	TOTAL MONEY
1	$500.00	$500.00	$5,500.00
2	$550.00	$1,050.00	$6,050.00
3	$605.00	$1,655.00	$6,655.00
...	...	...	...
20	$3,057.96	$28,637.55	$33,637.50

Here's how your earnings would stack up after 20 years in a regular brokerage account:

YEAR	THIS YEAR'S RETURN (AFTER TAXES)	TOTAL RETURNS	TOTAL MONEY
1	$490.00	$490.00	$5,490.00
2	$538.02	$1,028.02	$6,028.02
3	$590.75	$1,618.77	$6,618.77
...	...	...	...
20	$2,894.95	$27,435.22	$32,435.22

In a Roth IRA, the exact same investment would make you more than $1,200 more than it would in a brokerage account – with no extra work needed. If two people were offering you two different amounts to do the exact same task, why would you choose the person that's paying less?

This is more beneficial with a Roth IRA than a Traditional IRA. Mainly because you get to pay taxes on your investments before they grow and compound. Paying taxes on your investments after they've grown is often more costly than getting it out of the way on the front-end.

To take full advantage of the Roth IRA tax benefits, try to make sure the stocks you choose pay out dividends.

Note: revisit the section on dividend stocks in the Investing chapter for a refresher.

Where should you contribute?

In a perfect world, not only would you be able to buy mimosas at Waffle House, but you'd also be able to max out both your 401(k) and IRA contributions. This isn't realistic for most people. When it comes to prioritizing your retirement savings, here are the steps I recommend taking:

1) Contribute the most your company will match to your 401(k)

If your job matches 401(k) contributions, your first priority should be contributing the highest amount they'll match. If they match 3%, contribute 3%. If they match 6%, contribute 6%. If they don't match at all, start updating your resume – you don't want to be there too much longer.

Contributing anything less than the most your company will match is leaving free money on the table. I don't know about you, but I'm still ringing up organic produce in the self-checkout line as regular produce; I can't afford to leave free money out there.

2) Max out your IRA contributions

After your 401(k) is set to contribute your company's match, you want to begin contributing to your IRA. Mostly because of the huge selection of investment options available. Even if you have zero interest in all the options, at least use their big selection to access the cheap index funds offered. These may not be available in your 401(k) plan.

3) Return to your 401(k)

Once you've maxed out your IRA contributions, you should then consider increasing your 401(k) contributions. Even with higher fees and limited options, 401(k)s are still a great resource.

CHAPTER FIVE

STUDENT LOANS

"Will I make it from the student loans to a Benzo?"
—KANYE WEST

S tudy hard," they said. "Make good grades," they said. "Get into college," they said. "Graduate and get a good job," they said. Growing up, it seems that folks told us everything except the winning lottery numbers and how to properly fold a fitted sheet.

You wanna know what else a lot of those same folks failed to mention? The fact that chances are after you do everything they advised you to do, you'll be in so much debt that your paychecks will disappear right before your eyes like spinach when you cook it.

Yes, graduating from college can open the door for more job opportunities and the social experience can be priceless (and by priceless, I mean expensive). We've heard that our entire lives – we get it. But, who knew you'd have to pay an arm and a leg just to barely pay attention in lectures and sleep in twin beds that squeak if you even blink too hard?

Don't get the wrong impression, though, I'm not knocking college by any means. It's a great experience, and I wouldn't trade my college years for anything. But the student loan debt aspect of it is a harsh reality for most people.

In America, borrowers collectively owe $1.5 trillion in student loans. That's trillion with a 'T'. The problem of student loan debt is even more prominent within Black communities. Almost 78% of Black students borrow federal loans to pay for school, compared to around 58% of White students. To make matters worse, Black students are more likely to have trouble repaying the loan and often end up defaulting. Not only is this a byproduct of the wealth gap, but the problem in itself is also contributing to the wealth gap.

As with most things in life, though, the more you know, the better-suited you are to handle a situation.

Student loans fall into one of two categories: federal or private. Although they serve the same purpose, there are notable differences between them.

Federal loans come from Uncle Sam 'nem and usually offer lower interest rates and more flexible repayment plans. On the other hand, private loans come from banks, credit unions, or other financial institutions, and usually have higher interest rates.

FEDERAL LOANS

Federal loans, which should be your preference over private loans, will either be a part of the Direct Loan Program (commonly referred to as Stafford Loans) or the Federal Perkins Loan Program (referred to as Perkins Loans). These loans are not limited to four-year colleges or universities. They also cover the costs of community colleges, career schools, trade schools, and technical schools. If you want to get any type of post-high school education, there's a federal loan for you.

Before you can apply for any federal student aid, you must complete the Free Application for Federal Student Aid (FAFSA). It's not optional. The FAFSA application usually opens on October 1st of every year, so be sure to mark your calendars.

Direct Stafford Loans

The Direct Loan Program, which is most common, consists of four types of loans: direct subsidized, direct unsubsidized, direct PLUS, and direct consolidation.

- *Direct subsidized loans*: These are for the financially-challenged (a.k.a. broke), undergraduate students. If you never had to drink "Cola" instead of Coca-Cola, Mr. Pibb instead of Dr. Pepper, or "Lemon-Lime Soda" instead of Sprite growing up, then chances are you don't qualify for these loans.

  If no one in your family used to buy food stamps for cents on the dollar growing up, you probably don't qualify. If, "You got McDonald's money?" wasn't a question you heard frequently growing up, you probably don't qualify. As long as you're in school half-time, the federal government pays the interest on these loans. They will also cover the interest during the six-month grace period after you graduate, and during deferment periods.

- *Direct unsubsidized loans*: These loans are available to undergraduate, graduate, and professional students. You don't need to have financial needs to qualify. Even Hunter from the private Catholic school in the suburbs that paid $30 for grams of weed growing up is eligible. With these loans, it's on you to pay all of the interest — even as it accrues while you're in school and during deferment periods.

- *Direct PLUS loans*: These are available to graduate and professional students, as well as parents of dependent undergraduate students. If you fall in the parent category, you will be solely responsible for paying back the loan, even though it was taken out for the student's benefit. The intent is to offset expenses not covered by other financial aid. The maximum amount that you can receive is your cost of attendance minus all other financial aid that you've received. You will also need a good credit history to qualify.

- *Direct Consolidation loans*: These loans allow you to combine all of your federal loans into one loan, making it easier to keep up with.

Here is how subsidized and unsubsidized loans compare:

Subsidized

- Eligibility based on financial need.
- Only available to undergraduate students.
- You don't pay interest while you're in school at least half-time or during your grace period.

Unsubsidized

- Not based on financial need.
- Available to undergraduate and graduate students.
- Interest is charged as soon as the loan is dispersed.

Perkins Loans

Unlike Stafford Loans, Perkins Loans are low-interest federal loans that come from your school instead of Uncle Sam 'nem. Not every school offers this program, so be sure to check if yours does. You must be an undergraduate and graduate student with an exceptional financial need to qualify. If you've never been so broke that you had to borrow gas money just so you could drive somewhere to borrow money, then you probably don't qualify.

If you're attending school at least half-time, you'll have a nine-month grace period after you graduate, leave school, or drop below half-time status before you have to start paying back the loan. If you're attending school less than half-time, check with your school to check the length of your grace period, because it may vary.

Repayments for these loans will be made to the school that disbursed it.

PRIVATE LOANS

Private loans are the other option for those needing funding for school. However, it is strongly recommended that you consider private loans only after you've exhausted all your federal loan, scholarship, grant, and work-study options. If you go for private loans without trying all of those options, then you've sold yourself short.

Since private loans are made by corporations such as banks, credit unions, and various state-affiliated organizations, the terms and conditions of the loans can vary widely, as they're set by the lender. Regardless of the lender, you can expect to have higher interest rates than a federal loan.

Let's say that you've exhausted all of the aforementioned options, and your financial aid package is still not enough to cover the total cost. At that point, a private loan may be inevitable.

If you somehow find yourself in that situation, here are some things you should know about private loans:

- Private loans often require an established credit history. This won't be a huge problem for most people applying to graduate and professional school because they tend to be older. For most undergraduate students, however, this means you'll need a co-signer. For what it's worth, a good amount of private loan recipients have a co-signer. If the co-signer has good credit, then you could get a lower rate.

- Most private student loans have variable interest rates, meaning it could fluctuate during the span of the loan. You must be prepared to pay back more over time, if the rate goes up. That's just how the game goes.

- They may not offer deferments and forbearance. If you find yourself in a bind and you have federal loans, you typically have the option to pause or temporarily reduce your payments while you get back on your feet. With private loans, this may not be an option. Private lenders are way less understanding when it comes to hardships. They couldn't care less about what you're going through — they need that bread up off you.

• No income-based repayment plans. There are a lot of people struggling to make ends meet, and having a high ass student loan payment obviously doesn't help. With federal loans, you can rely on income-based plans to cap your monthly payment at a certain amount. This isn't the case with private student loans.

Here is how federal loans compare to private loans:

Federal

- Fixed loan interest rates.
- Interest rate not based on credit score.
- Eligible for loan forgiveness.
- Income-based repayment plans available.
- Able to defer payments for unemployment or hardships.

Private

- Can have fixed or variable interest rates.
- Interest rate determined by credit score.
- Not eligible for loan forgiveness.
- Income-based repayments plans are usually not an option.
- Deferment may not be an option.

FUTURE COLLEGE STUDENTS (AND THEIR PARENTS)

It doesn't matter if your parents are tech billionaires, professional athletes, cashiers at Walmart (who apparently never work because there's always 100 lanes in Walmart with only two ever open), or burger flippers at McDonald's, your second priority should be completing the FAFSA. Your first priority, of course, should be on getting good grades and all that good stuff, but outside of that, your focus should be on completing the FAFSA. Even if you don't qualify for the income-based aid, at least put yourself in position to receive *something*.

Knowing the difference between loan types will be important to understand when determining which kind of aid you should accept and how much.

It's equally important to understand your financial aid "award" letter.

Don't let the name fool you. Your financial aid award is usually not much of an award. Schools typically combine your scholarship and grant money with loans to make your aid package total seem bigger. Don't fall for the okey doke. Be sure to know exactly how much of your aid comes from loans and how much comes from scholarships and grants.

CURRENT COLLEGE STUDENTS

Balancing classes, extra-curriculars, family obligations, and social life is a hard-enough task on its own; the last thing college students should be worried about is the lump sum of debt waiting for them at the end like the finish line tape at track meets. Imagine Sallie Mae holding one end of the tape, and Uncle Sam holding the other.

Unfortunately, thinking about this debt is a reality for many students. Especially during senior year. As your college years start winding down, there are some things you should begin to do:

- Know your grace period. You'll normally have six-months after you graduate, before you have to start making payments. The exception is a PLUS loan, which begins when it's disbursed. With private loans, the grace period could vary by lender so double-check to be sure.

- Know who you owe and how much. Seems obvious, I know, but you'd be surprised at how many people graduate and don't know this information. Be sure to know who you owe because when your grace period is over, you can damn sure believe they'll know you.

- Focus on what's important. Trust me, you'll have plenty of time after graduation to worry about debt and all of that. Don't spoil the last of those college golden years worrying about the inevitable. Use that energy for something worthwhile.

AFTER SCHOOL

You did it. You came, you saw, and you [hopefully] conquered. Chances are that you paid a hell of a lot of money to do it, too. You might've gone on to corporate America, went to graduate school, or you might've moved back home to figure out your next move. Hell, you might've not even finished school (life happens). No matter the path, there's one common denominator — whoever lent you money for school is going to want it back.

Just like chances are high that you won't actually get a call back when a Black person tells you, "I'ma call you back," chances are equally high that most of your peers have student loan debt as well, so don't feel bad.

And just like it's likely that a White man with a buzz cut wearing a pair of Oakley's is the police, it's likely that your peers are as confused about student loans as you are.

Repayment

After a while, the inevitable happens. Your grace period runs out, and it's time to start repaying your loan.

Because federal loans offer more flexible repayment plans, it's important to find the repayment plan that's right for you. There are eight types of repayment plans offered — four of which are income-based. The repayment plan can be changed so don't worry about being stuck with it.

You'll automatically be placed on the standard repayment plan, which has fixed monthly payments. There's also a graduated repayment plan where your payments will be lower initially and increase over time. The length of these loans is 10 years (30 if your loans are consolidated). There's also an extended repayment plan, which can have fixed or graduated payments, with a term period of 25 years.

The income-based plans are...well...based on your income. Your monthly payments will be determined by a percentage of your **discretionary income** — which is the money you have left over after you pay for essential expenses like rent, utilities, and food. The monthly amount you pay will never be more than you would pay on a 10-year standard plan, but you will typically pay more over time.

Your payment amount is re-calculated each year, and is based on your income and family size. You have to update this information annually, even if it hasn't changed.

Any outstanding balance you have on your loan will be forgiven after 20 years or 25 years (depending on when you received the first loan). Chances are that you'll have to pay income tax on the forgiven amount, though.

Consolidation

Unfortunately, most folks are forced to take out multiple loans to cover their schooling expenses. Keeping up with these loans — their payment amounts, due dates, interest rates, etc. — can become a bigger hassle than driving in Atlanta during rush hour. This is where loan consolidation comes into play. Loan consolidation allows you to combine your multiple student loans into one single loan.

If you only have federal loans, you can combine them into a Direct Consolidation Loan. You won't necessarily receive a better interest rate because your new rate will be averaged, but you will have the convenience of a single loan and access to additional repayment plans and loan forgiveness programs.

Consolidating your loans can lower your monthly payment by giving you more time (up to 30 years) to pay the debt back. This is a gift and a curse, because you'll likely pay more in interest over the life of the loan.

When it comes to private student loans, consolidation is usually done in conjunction with refinancing. Student loan refinancing is similar to loan consolidation in that they both combine multiple loans into one new loan. The key difference with refinancing, however, is that it involves issuing a completely new loan with a better interest rate.

For example, if you have a $14,000 loan with 7% interest and a $6,000 loan with 9% interest, you could refinance and get a single $20,000 loan with a 4% rate. You'll still owe the same amount, just with less interest.

You should consider refinancing your private loans if:

- Your credit has risen noticeably since you originally received your loan. You'll want a credit score of at least 700, to be safe. It's easier to push furniture through sand than it is getting approved with a less-than-good credit score.

- You have a stable job and steady income.

- You've been making your payments on-time since leaving school.

If you don't fall into those three categories, your only hope is finding a co-signer who does.

If you refinance your federal loans then you lose certain benefits, such as the income-based plans and loan forgiveness programs. You should consider whether you need either of those, before making that move.

Deferment and forbearance

We all know how life can be. I get it, you get it, and fortunately for a lot of people, federal loan providers get it. This is why they offer deferments and forbearance. These allow you to temporarily lower or stop your federal loan repayments when times get rough.

The key difference between deferment and forbearance is that during the deferment period you won't be responsible for paying the interest that accumulates. You'll be responsible for the interest during forbearance.

Loan Forgiveness

In certain situations, you can have your federal loans forgiven. The most common ways are through the Public Service Loan Forgiveness (PSLF) program, which is for government and non-profit workers, and through the Teacher Loan Forgiveness program.

- Public Service Loan Forgiveness

Through the PSLF program, your loans are forgiven after you've made 120 qualifying payments under an income-based repayment plan. A qualifying payment is a payment of the *full* amount due, no later than 15 days after the due date, while employed full-time.

Payments while in school, during the grace period, and during deferment or forbearance don't qualify. The payments also don't have to be consecutive to count.

- Teacher Loan Forgiveness

Under the Teacher Loan Forgiveness Program (TLFP), you can have up to $17,500 of your loans forgiven if you teach for five complete and consecutive years at a low-income school. The U.S. Department of Education publishes a list of designated low-income schools every year, so be sure to check if your school qualifies.

- Perkins Loan Cancellation

If you have a Perkins Loan, you could be eligible for a loan cancellation for teaching full-time at a low-income school, or for teaching specific subjects. Minimum time required is only one full school year, but the longer you teach, the more of your loan that will be canceled. For a Perkins Loan cancellation, contact the financial aid office at the school that issued your loan to apply for cancellation.

CHAPTER SIX

TAXES

"On my way to Aspen, I forgot to do my taxes /
Call up my accountant, he gon' make it do magic."
—FUTURE

Other than getting 5 pieces in your 4-Piece Chicken Supremes Combo from Bojangles, few things bring more joy than payday. You've worked hard (and by worked hard, I mean probably did the bare minimum) and now it's time to finally get what you're owed. Unfortunately, by the time your paycheck hits your account, it's been Freddy Krueger sliced up. That's just how the game goes. Everybody knows that you pay taxes to the Internal Revenue Service ("IRS"), but to many, the process of taxation is confusing.

The amount of income taxes that you pay is primarily based on how much money you make. The United States uses a progressive income tax system. The more money that you make, the more taxes you pay (or at least that's how it's supposed to work). Your tax bracket is the highest tax rate you'll have to pay on your income and is determined by your taxable income. Your taxable income may vary from your regular income as it can include tax credits, deductions, and exclusions. For example, if you make $60,000 per year but have $10,000 in tax deductions, only $50,000 will be taxable.

As of 2019, there are seven marginal income tax brackets: 10%, 12%, 22%, 24%, 32%, 35%, and 37%.

2019 INDIVIDUAL TAX BRACKETS			
TAX RATE	SINGLE	MARRIED FILING JOINTLY	HEAD OF HOUSEHOLD
10%	0 to $9,700	0 to $19,400	0 to $13,850
12%	$9,701 to $39,475	$19,401 to $78,950	$13,851 to $52,850
22%	$39,476 to $84,200	$78,951 to $168,400	$52,851 to $84,200
24%	$84,201 to $160,725	$168,401 to $321,450	$84,201 to $160,700
32%	$160,726 to $204,100	$321,451 to $408,200	$160,701 to $204,100
35%	$204,101 to $510,300	$408,201 to $612,350	$204,101 to $510,300
37%	$510,301+	$612,351+	$510,301+

A common misconception is that your income is taxed at whatever percentage your bracket is. That's not quite how it works. Different portions of your income are taxed at different rates.

For example, let's imagine that you're single and make $50,000 per year. Instead of all of your income being taxed at 22%, it will be taxed at the following:

- The first $9,700 will be taxed at 10%.
- $9,701 through $39,475 will be taxed at 12%.
- $39,476 to $50,000 will be taxed at 22%.

Instead of paying $11,000 in taxes ($50,000 * 22%), you will only pay $6,858.50:

$9,700 * 10% = $970.
$29,775 * 12% = $3,573.
$10,525 * 22% = $2,315.50.

A big reason behind this is to provide more equality in the tax assessment. As a result, someone who may fall into a particular bracket by only a few hundred dollars doesn't have to potentially pay thousands more in taxes. Imagine making $40,000 and having to pay 22% in taxes versus someone who makes $39,000 paying 12%:

$40,000 * 22% = $8,800
$39,000 * 12% = $4,680

If I were the person making $40,000, I'd be pissed. That might be the only time in life that I'd request a pay cut. Luckily, this isn't how it works.

The majority of companies will automatically have taxes deducted from your paychecks and sent to the IRS for you. If you're self-employed, it's expected that you pay income tax on a quarterly basis.

If, at the end of the year, you didn't pay enough to cover your total income tax due, you'll owe the IRS the remaining amount. If you paid too much, the IRS will send you what's owed via a tax refund.

FILING TAXES

The time has finally come. All year, Uncle Sam has been dippin' into your checks, and now the time has come to get back what's rightfully yours. Or, unfortunately for some people, pay back what you owe. And trust me, you're gonna want to do that sooner rather than later.

Before filing taxes, the two things you want to do are make sure you need to file (there's a very, very good chance that you do) and get your paperwork together.

If you're single and make over $10,350 per year, then you must file. If you're married, filing jointly, and the household income is over $20,700, then you must file. If you're a dependent and made over $6,300, then you must file — no exceptions.

Form 1040 is the standard Federal income tax form you file that reports your pre-tax income. Prior to the 2018 tax year, there were different types of 1040 forms depending on your situation, but for the sake of simplicity, a new 1040 form was created that allows all taxpayers to use the same form.

As tax season approaches, you can expect to start receiving various income-reporting forms. Here are five common tax forms that you're liable to run into at some point:

1) W-2. This is by far the most common form. It shows the amount that you earned during the calendar year, as well as the taxes withheld by your employer. Your employer must send this form to you and the IRS at the end of each year.

2) 1099. If you did freelance work, consultant work, or a side gig — like driving for Uber or Lyft — and received more than $600 in compensation, you'll receive one of these forms. If you earned less than $600, I'm going to pray it was strictly a side hustle and not what you relied on to keep the rent paid. If you made less than $600, you won't get a 1099 form, but you will still have to report that income.

3) 1098-E. If your student loan provider seemingly put on a ski mask and robbed you for more than $600 in interest on your student loan payments in the previous year, you'll receive one of these forms from your loan provider.

4) 1098-T. If you're enrolled in higher education, you'll receive this form from your school. It will show the amount that you paid (or were billed for) in qualified educational expenses that year. Qualified educational expenses will include tuition, fees, required coursework material, and other related costs required for enrollment. Room and board, transportation, student health fees, and similar personal living expenses are not included.

5) 1099-B. You'll receive this form if you made any stock transactions during the previous year. It should report the amount gained/lost from the sale of stocks and should be sent to you automatically by your broker.

DEDUCTIONS AND TAX CREDITS

In addition to the tax forms you should automatically be receiving, you should also gather documentation for any deductions and tax credits that you may qualify for. The primary difference between them is that deductions lower your taxable income, while tax credits reduce what you owe in taxes.

For example, if you made $60,000, a $5,000 deduction would mean only $55,000 is taxable. On the other end, a $5,000 tax credit would be added to your return (or subtracted from what you owe). Unfortunately, people often miss out on deductions and tax credits because they don't know about them.

The IRS gives you two choices: take a standard deduction or itemize your deductions. You can't do both.

The standard deduction is a flat amount that the IRS lets you deduct from your taxable income, zero questions asked. As of 2019, the amounts are:

Single or married people filing separately: $12,000
Married filing jointly: $24,000

Single filer with dependents: $18,000

If you're married but file separately and your spouse chooses to itemize their deductions, you can't take the standard deduction. You both have to choose the standard deduction.

Itemizing your deductions isn't a walk in the park. It requires writing out all of your deductible expenses. Of course, you must be able to provide evidence for what you're claiming. Lying about your child's age at a restaurant so that they can eat for the kids' price is perfectly fine; lying to Uncle Sam about deductions is not.

For the average person without a mortgage, it's likely that you'd want to go with the standard deduction because it's simple and is probably more than you'd get from adding up your deductions.

You may want to consider itemizing your deductions if:

- You paid interest on a mortgage and property taxes,
- You made a large charitable donation, or
- You had large out-of-pocket expenses.

If you decide to go the itemize route, here are some deductions to consider:

Earned Income Tax Credit (EITC): This tax credit is meant to ease the tax pain for folks with lower-ish income (typically $55,000 or less). The credit starts around $500 and goes up to more than $6,000 — depending on how many children you have and your filing status. You can't take the credit if you're married and filing separately, and the claimed children must be under 19 (24 if they're a full-time student).

Charitable donation: The majority of donations made to charities can be deducted. You shouldn't make donations for the sake of writing it off on your taxes, of course. However, if you're going to make them, you might as well reap the rewards, right? Be sure to keep a record of who you donated to, when you donated, and how much you donated.

Medical expenses: You can usually deduct any out-of-pocket medical expenses that are more than 7.5% of your income. For example, if you make $50,000, you can deduct anything exceeding $3,750. If your bill is $5,000, $1,250 can be deducted. A few states have a different percentage threshold, so be sure to double-check.

Children: If you're a parent or guardian, you can receive up to $2,000 in tax credits per child (under 17 years old). You can also get a tax credit for daycare (or anything similar) through the childcare tax credit. It allows you to claim up to $3,000 in care expenses for one child younger than 12 years old, and up to $6,000 if you have two or more children.

Unlike the child tax credit, the childcare tax credit also applies if you're paying someone to take care of an aging or disabled parent/relative.

Job Search: As if being unemployed wasn't bad enough, the costs associated with job searching can creep up on you like a Jehovah's Witness when they see you with your door open. Fortunately, you can deduct a lot of these expenses — including travel costs (transportation, lodging, and meals), employment agency fees, and costs associated with preparing and mailing off your resume. As with most things, there are some exceptions:

- The job search must be in your current line of work. If you're a plumber, you can't expect to deduct expenses while looking for an investment banking job.
- You can't be looking for your first job.
- It can't be a long gap between your last job and your job search.

SELF-EMPLOYED

A lot of people dream of one day being their own boss. You have some folks doing freelance graphic design, some doing consultancy, and some selling clip art graphics on plain t-shirts. Whatever the case, you're going to run into expenses along the way. Being self-employed comes with some valuable tax deductions and credits. Here are some deductions to be aware of:

Home office: It's very common for self-employed folks to do their work from their house. If you have a home office and do a large amount of your business there, you may be eligible for some deductions. The amount you can deduct depends on the size of your workspace compared to the size of your house. If your home office takes up 15% of your house (based on square footage), you can write off 15% of certain expenses — including rent, renter's or homeowner's insurance, and utilities.

The other option is to deduct a flat amount (usually $5) per square foot of your home office. Depending on the size of your office, this option may get you a lower deduction, but it's a much simpler alternative because you don't have to keep as many records.

You may also deduct the cost of supplies for your home office. Bought a desk? Deduct it. Bought a printer? Deduct it. Bought some index cards? Deduct it. You can also deduct a laptop or tablet if you're using it predominantly for business.

Health insurance: If you bought health insurance for you and your family, you may be able to deduct the cost. If your spouse has health insurance through their job and you're eligible to join their plan but choose not to, you won't be able to take this deduction. The deduction also can't exceed the amount you made that year.

Travel: If you're self-employed, you can deduct a set amount per every mile that you drive for business purposes. It doesn't matter if you're driving to Magic City in Atlanta to meet with a client (business is business, right?) or driving to the local Staples for office supplies. It's deductible.

If you're traveling for business, you can also deduct costs such as the plane ticket, hotel, Uber/Lyft costs, and parking. This, of course, is assuming you did "business" that day. Business tends to be relative, so take that how you want.

You can also deduct a portion of your meals and some entertainment costs, as long as you did business before, during, or after the event. How convenient would it be to have a "business meeting" before the NBA Finals?

Education: You can deduct tuition, books, fees, and other similar things for any work-related education expenses that you paid during the year. The education has to benefit you in your present work; you can't take classes to change careers. Don't expect to be working in sales getting your pre-med classes paid for.

Retirement: One of the biggest perks of working for a corporation is the 401(k)-plan offered. As a self-employed person, you now have the option of opening a solo 401(k) plan. It works much like a traditional 401(k) — the contributions are pre-tax, there are contribution limits, and there are penalties for early withdrawals.

As with anything tax-related, the key is to keep all receipts and documentation related to your deductions and be honest with your claims. You may think you can get over on Uncle Sam but eventually, it will catch up to you. It always does.

DECIDE HOW YOU'RE GONNA FILE

After you've gathered all of your paperwork, the next step is deciding how to file. The deadline to file your taxes is April 15th. If April 15th happens to fall on a weekend or holiday, the deadline will be the next business day.

The method you choose to file your taxes should depend on how complicated your financial situation is. If you're single, no dependents, don't own a house, and only have a few forms, save yourself the trouble (and money) and use a tax software program or an app. The same applies if you're employed with a little side hustle, but not much more. As a note, the IRS has free filing software for people with income below a certain amount.

If you run your own business, have investments, own property, etc., it may be in your best interest to get a tax professional because of the potential complexity. They will help make sure that the information is filed correctly and can help maximize your return. They're generally the most expensive option, but you'll be thankful that you paid the fee.

If you make under $54,000, have a disability, or speak limited English, you can get free in-person tax help via the Volunteer Income Tax Assistance (VITA) program. VITA sites are usually located at community centers, schools, libraries, and other convenient locations. You can check the IRS website to find a VITA site near you.

FILL-OUT, REVIEW, FILE

The hard part is over. You've got your files together. You've filled out everything that you needed to. Now, all you have to do is review everything and file.

If you owe the IRS money, your next step is to decide how you're going to pay them. If you're gonna be receiving tax money back, all you can do at this time is wait for your money. The IRS alleges that 90% of returns filed will be delivered within 21 days. If you're like me, it'd be just your luck to be in that 10%, but I'll keep my fingers crossed for you.

CHAPTER SEVEN

BUDGETING

"I'm just a, big bang baller on a budget."
—Nappy Roots

The word 'budget' always seems to have a negative connotation surrounding it. When people hear it, they think of restrictions and limitations. Similar to when people hear the word 'diet'. It's like once you get on a budget or a diet, your mind automatically focuses on the things you can't spend money on, or the food that you can't eat.

Budgeting doesn't have to mean going on a rice and tap water diet, or wearing coats in the house during the winter to avoid turning the heat on. You don't have to turn into Mr. Krabs or anything like that, fam. More than anything, budgeting is about being aware. Your budget can be as strict as African parents, or it can be as lenient as Walmart's return policy. The choice is yours.

There's no magic formula or hidden secret to budgeting effectively. Most people know how to set up a basic budget — the problem is following it. The intentions are good; the execution is just flawed. It's like when you buy a bunch of produce at the grocery store thinking you're going to be extra healthy, only to end up throwing most of it away because you let it spoil.

More than anything, the problem is a person's mindset. Instead of thinking of planning your finances as budgeting, think of it as a spending plan. On the surface, a budget and a spending plan are incredibly similar, but there's one key difference: the psychology behind it.

With a budget, it can often feel like your money is controlling you, and you have to go through life being defensive with your spending.

With a spending plan, you become the quarterback. Of course you'd rather be Tom Brady than Mark Sanchez, but nonetheless, a spending plan puts you in charge of your money and lets you decide where it would most benefit you. Instead of focusing on where you have to cut back on your monthly spending, you focus on your big picture financial goals and decide how your money will best help you accomplish them.

Regardless of the method that you take, there are a few surface level things you need to know like the back of your hand: how much you make, how much you spend, and your goals (both savings and debt pay-off).

Income: Unless you're a freelancer where your monthly income can widely vary from month-to-month, you should know exactly how much money you bring in monthly. It doesn't matter if it's from a salary, flippin' dime bags, child support, or investments. Count it all and write it down. If your income isn't consistent, then use your average income from the last six months.

Expenses: When it comes to your expenses, divide them into two categories: needs and wants.

- Needs are: Rent, utilities, groceries, healthcare, insurance, and basic clothing.
- Wants are: Phone, cable, entertainment, vacations, and non-basic clothing. If you have to question whether it's a want or need, it's probably a want.

Not only does having your needs and wants separate help with setting a budget, but it also makes you aware of just how much of your expenses you could get rid of if shit hits the fan and you need to shift into full-blown survival mode.

A good tip is to add about 10% to your total expenses to give yourself breathing room for unexpected expenses. Nobody thinks they'll experience an unexpected expense until they experience an unexpected expense. That's just how it goes. If your monthly expenses are $1,500, write down $1,650. If they're $2,000, write down $2,200.

Goals: when it comes to your financial goals, you want to have a savings goal and a debt pay-off goal (if you have debt). Goals are going to be important to your spending plan. They should fall into one of three categories:

- Less than three months,
- Three months to a year, or
- More than a year.

It doesn't matter what these goals are, just make sure that they're actual goals of yours. It doesn't matter if you think it's a "bad" goal, write it down. If you write down something that's not an actual goal of yours, working towards it is going to seem like a chore — which defeats the purpose. Your goals could be:

Less than three months:
- A new Gucci bag and to get your cracked iPhone screen fixed so you can stop cutting your thumb every time you try to unlock it.

Three months to a year
- A new laptop and three months of rent in savings.

More than a year
- Money for a mortgage deposit and a trip to China.

After you have your goals, you need to write down your priorities. Along with your needs, your priorities may (and probably should) include things like saving for retirement, having an emergency fund in place, saving for your child's college, etc.

Once you have this in place, your task is to allocate your income. With a budget, you typically look at your finances from a month-to-month view. The purpose of the spending plan is to look at the big picture of your finances. You identify what really matters to you and use your money accordingly.

Here are steps you can take to make your spending plan:

1) Write down all of your expenses, goals, and priorities (in the order of their importance).

2) Take your monthly income and "spend" it towards the things identified in the step above. You don't have to "spend" it all, but everything listed should have *something* put towards it – no matter how small.

3) Use whatever is left however you see fit.

It's really that simple. There's no setting category amounts and then spending the money down like a traditional budget. You prioritize things that matter to you and then have the freedom to use the rest however you want.

However, if you're a person that prefers a bit more structure, here are some broad budget structures you can use to create your budget.

BALANCED MONEY FORMULA

This type of budget follows a 50-30-20 rule that recommends allocating 50% of your income to needs, 30% to wants, and 20% to savings. These percentages aren't written in stone, but they're a good foundation. More than a monthly budget, the Balanced Money Formula is a goal. You eventually want to get to the point where you can follow the 50-30-20 rule.

For example, if you bring in $2,000 monthly, only $1,000 should be spent on needs, $600 should go to wants, and $400 should go to savings. That's not very realistic for most people. With rent prices higher than a '70s hippie nowadays, by the time that you pay rent and buy a few canned goods, you could very well be over 50%.

You should know what your current percentages are now and then start planning on what you can do to get them to 50-30-20. For some folks, all it takes is a change in a few priorities. However, it's not that easy for most people. If you're bringing in $2,000 monthly but have $1,500 in needs, not having money for savings isn't because your priorities are off, it's because of life. Anybody who preaches anything different deserves to be smacked with the might of Zeus.

If your needs are high, making a noticeable change usually requires finding a better paying job or moving somewhere cheaper. Neither of which is simple. If it were that easy, everybody would be doing it.

If your needs are 50%, but your wants are 40-45%, that's a different story. That can normally be adjusted by re-evaluating your lifestyle.

ZERO-BASED BUDGETING

The purpose of this method is to make sure every dollar you bring in monthly is accounted for, at the beginning of the month. This doesn't mean spend everything you bring in (that would defeat the purpose), it means that at the beginning of the month you should have a destination for every dime of income that you have.

Unlike the Balanced Money Formula, it's not as simple as broad categories getting assigned a percentage of your paycheck and then using that amount however you see fit. It's about knowing how much you're going to spend on what, before the month even begins.

If after your expenses you have $500 left over, you need to know exactly how you're going to use that $500. You may decide to allocate $150 for savings, $100 for debt reduction, $100 for eating out, $100 for partying, and $50 for investing. It doesn't matter how you decide to divide it up. What matters is that you know where your money is going at the beginning of the month.

Unexpected expenses can pop up on you like a PETA activist, and some things you can't plan for, so keep that in mind when deciding how to allocate your money.

VALUE-BASED BUDGETING

Just like you can count on White people calling a predominantly Black neighborhood "sketchy," you can count on people spending outside of their budget. That's just how it tends to go. Value-based budgeting makes sure that your spending and saving habits align with what you value in life. Even if this method doesn't help you save money, at least the money you're spending will be on things you give a damn about, and not just spending for the sake of spending.

If you love traveling, you can justify paying $400 for a flight before you can justify spending $400 for a section in the club to party with the same folks you see every time you go out.

If you value experiences and love partying, you can justify spending that $400 in the club before you can justify spending $400 on a pair of shoes you heard your favorite rapper mention in a song.

Here are steps to take to set-up your budget:

1) List your values. Be honest with yourself, fam. If you value traveling and new experiences, write down traveling and new experiences. If you value expensive clothes and jewelry, write down expensive clothes and jewelry. No need to sugarcoat it. If you can't be real with yourself, who can you be real with? Write down at least three values.

2) Set one goal for each listed value. If you value traveling, visiting Africa might be a goal. If you value expensive clothes, buying a new Burberry jacket you seen one of the international students on campus wearing might be a goal. If you value family, sending your parents on a cruise might be a goal. It really doesn't matter. Your values, your goals.

3) Check your previous expenses. Add up all of your expenses that weren't a bill, savings, or fall under one of your values. The easiest way to do this is to get a bank statement and physically go through it, marking the expenses. If this is too much work for you, you're probably not as serious about budgeting as you think you are. (Somebody had to say it).

4) Re-allocate the money. Divide the total from #3 between the goals you listed in #2.

This method can help you put some of that "pointless" spending towards more meaningful things.

CASH-ONLY STRATEGY

This method is a method where you...well...only use cash. It's one thing to keep swiping a piece of plastic and not realize you've overspent until you get hit with the ever-so-humbling, "sorry, your card was declined" while the most attractive person in the store is standing behind you in line. I'm not saying this has happened to me or anything, I'm just saying that I've had to put a $4.02 pack of chicken back in the freezer, and grab the $3.98 pack to make sure that I had enough.

It's a different ball game to witness your money disappearing before your eyes every time you spend. This tends to make people reconsider questionable purchases.

Here are the steps that you should take to setup your cash-only budget:

1) Write down the amount you have remaining after your expenses and savings.

2) Take this amount out in cash.

3) Create subcategories for the money in #2. It could be "eating out," "shopping," "entertainment," etc. You decide which subcategories make the most sense for you, based on your lifestyle.

4) Divide the cash between the subcategories. I recommended getting some envelopes and having each one represent a different subcategory. Put the designated amount into the appropriate envelope and only spend what's in there. Once it's done, it's done.

PAY YOURSELF FIRST

This method is also referred to as the "80/20 budget." It's a simple way of budgeting that involves automatically setting aside 20% of your paycheck for savings, before you spend a dime. Hence the name "pay yourself first." If you can't afford the 20%, you can always lower the percentage, but try not to go too much lower. If anything, try to increase the percentage if you can reasonably afford to. The concept is based on the fact that you are far more likely to save money if you do this first. If you wait until all of your bills are paid, you are more likely to spend that money instead of saving. Pay Yourself First is more of a budgeting principle and could be applied to any of the strategies provided.

Here's how you should go about setting up this budget:

1) Write down your monthly income. Once you have this number, find out how much 20% of it is. If you bring in $3,000 monthly, write down $600.

2) Write down savings goals you have for different areas of your life. It could be for retirement, a new car, a house down payment, an emergency fund, or whatever.

3) Divide the 20% between your savings goals however you see fit. If $600 is your 20%, you can choose to divide it like this, for example:

- Retirement savings: $100
- House down payment: $200
- Vacation: $150
- Emergency fund: $150

There's no right or wrong way. Just make sure that you have your goals identified so that you can better allocate your money. If you're 21 years old, you would probably want to put more money towards a shorter-term goal like buying a car than you would towards retirement.

Again, it's one thing to sit down and write out a budget and have it look good on paper. It's a completely different thing to actually follow your budget in real life.

When thinking about saving money, don't just view it as something you're doing because you're *supposed* to. Think about specific financial goals that you're working towards. With this view, you're not "just saving money," you're putting money towards a goal that you have in mind. Just that little shift in mindset can help make budgeting purposeful, instead of a mandatory chore.

DON'T FORGET THE EMERGENCY FUND

The first thing I always encourage is for people to prioritize an emergency fund. You should have at least three months of living expenses saved, but six should be the goal. Going into your retirement accounts — like your 401(k) — is costly and usually not worth the taxes and penalties you'll pay for a withdrawal. If you ever lose your job, God forbid, that emergency fund is your lifeline while you're figuring out your next move. Please make it a priority. I'm Keith Sweat begging you!

"A wise person should have money in their head, but not in their heart."
—Jonathan Swift

DEBT VALIDATION LETTER TEMPLATE

Your Name
Your address
Your city, State, Zip Code

Name of Collector
Collector's Address
Collector's City, State, Zip Code

Date

To Whom It May Concern,

This letter is being sent to you in response to a notice sent to me on [*date the collector first contacted you*]. Be advised this is not a refusal to pay, but a notice sent pursuant to the Fair Debt Collection Practices Act, stating your claim is disputed and validation is requested.

This is not a request for verification or proof of my mailing address, but a request for validation. I respectfully request your offices provide me with competent evidence that I have any legal obligation to pay you.

At this time I will also inform you that if your offices have reported invalidated information to any of the 3 major credit bureaus (Equifax, Experian or TransUnion) this action might constitute fraud under both Federal and State laws. Including: violation of the *Fair Credit Reporting Act*, violation of the *Fair Debt Collection Practices Act*, and *Defamation of Character*.

If your offices are able to provide the proper documentation as requested in the following Declaration, I will require at least 30 days to investigate this information, during which time all collection activity must **cease and desist.** Also during this validation period, if any action is taken which could be considered detrimental to any of my credit reports, I will consult with my legal counsel for suit.

This includes any listing of any information to a credit-reporting agency that could be inaccurate or invalidated. If your office fails to respond to this validation request within 30 days from the date of your receipt, all references to this account must be deleted and completely removed from my credit file and a copy of such deletion request shall be sent to me immediately.

I would also like to request, in writing, that your offices make no further telephone contact to me. If your offices continue to attempt telephone communication with me it will be considered harassment and I will have no choice but to file suit. All future communications with me must be done in writing and sent to the address noted in this letter.

Sincerely,
Your Name

CREDIT REPORT DISPUTE TEMPLATE

Your Name
Your Address
Your City, State, Zip Code

Name of Credit Bureau and Department
Credit Bureau Address
Credit Bureau City, State, Zip Code

Date

To Whom It May Concern,

I am writing to dispute the following information in my file. The items I dispute are also encircled on the attached copy of my report.

This/these item(s) [identify item(s) disputed by name of source, such as creditors and identify type of item, such as credit account] is/are inaccurate because [*describe what is inaccurate and why*]. I am requesting that the item be deleted (or request another specific change) to correct the information.

Enclosed are copies of [*describe any documents included, such as payment records, court documents, etc.*] supporting my position. Please re-investigate this/these matter(s) and [*delete or correct*] the disputed item(s) as soon as possible.

Sincerely,
Your Name
Your birthdate

Enclosed: [*list items you are enclosing*]
For identity purposes, you're going to want to include a copy of your drivers license, a copy of your social security card, and a utility-like bill with your name on it

ENDNOTES

Introduction

- Census data from Current Population Survey 2010 (family wealth)
- "The Road to Zero Wealth: How the racial wealth divide is hollowing out America's middle class" (Asanta-Muhammad, Collins, Hoxie, Nieves, *Institute for Policy Studies & Prosperity Now*, 2017)

Chapter One. Credit

- https://www.nationwide.com/car-insurance-credit-score.jsp
- https://www.experian.com/blogs
- https://www.valuepenguin.com/average-credit-score

Chapter Two. Credit Cards

- https://www.americanexpress.com
- https://www.capitalone.com
- https://www.citi.com

Chapter Three. Investing

- https://www.zillow.com/home-values/
- https://www.macrotrends.net/2324/sp-500-historical-chart-data

Chapter Four. Retirement

- https://www.irs.gov/retirement-plans/2019-ira-deduction-limits-effect-of-modified-agi-on-deduction-if-you-are-covered-by-a-retirement-plan-at-work
- https://www.irs.gov/retirement-plans/2019-ira-deduction-limits-effect-of-modified-agi-on-deduction-if-you-are-not-covered-by-a-retirement-plan-at-work
- https://www.irs.gov/retirement-plans/amount-of-roth-ira-contributions-that-you-can-make-for-2019
- https://www.irs.gov/newsroom/401k-contribution-limit-increases-to-19000-for-2019-ira-limit-increases-to-6000

Chapter Five. Student Loans

- https://www.marketwatch.com/story/student-debt-just-hit-15-trillion-2018-05-08
- https://www.nerdwallet.com/blog/loans/student-loans/black-student-debt-crisis/
- https://studentaid.ed.gov/sa/repay-loans/understand/plans
- https://studentaid.ed.gov/sa/types/loans

Chapter Six. Taxes

- https://www.irs.gov/newsroom/irs-provides-tax-inflation-adjustments-for-tax-year-2019

- https://www.irs.gov/credits-deductions/individuals/earned-income-tax-credit/eitc-income-limits-maximum-credit-amounts

Chapter Seven. Budgeting

- Warren, E., Tyagi, A. (2006). *All Your Worth: The Ultimate Lifetime Money Plan*

ABOUT THE AUTHOR

STEFON WALTERS is an Oodles O' Noodles con-
noisseur turned financial literacy advocate. With a
knack for seamlessly connecting the worlds of finance and entertainment, he's a breath of fresh air
in an often dull industry. He currently resides in Los
Angeles where he spends a lot of his time teaching
finance topics in a way many find enjoyable and re-
freshing. *Finessin' Finances* is his debut novel.

CONNECT

Twitter: **@WaltD336**

Instagram: **@WaltD336**

Email: **stefon@finessinfinances.com**

stefonwalters.com

38218570R00086

Made in the USA
Middletown, DE
07 March 2019